A CELEBRANT'S GUIDE TO THE NEW SACRAMENTARY

A Cycle

Kevin W. Irwin

PUEBLO PUBLISHING COMPANY

NEW YORK

Nihil Obstat:

William B. Smith, S.T.D.
Censor Deputatus

Imprimatur:

✝ James P. Mahoney
*Vicar General,
Archdiocese of New York*

Design: Frank Kacmarcik, D. F. A.

The text of The New American Bible, copyright © 1970 by the Confraternity of Christian Doctrine, Washington, D. C. (Books 1 Samuel to 2 Maccabees, 1969) is reproduced herein by license of said Confraternity of Christian Doctrine. All rights reserved.

Copyright © 1975, Pueblo Publishing Company, Inc., 1860 Broadway, New York, New York 10023. All rights reserved. Manufactured in U. S. A.

DEDICATION

To my mother and brother, in memory of my father.

AUTHOR'S PREFACE

Many people have been instrumental in aiding the author in the publication of this volume. Thanks are due primarily to the Reverend Monsignor Myles M. Bourke for recommending the author for the task of writing this commentary, and to Mr. Bernard Benziger for his assistance and encouragement in its preparation. For her secretarial help and long hours of typing the manuscript the author wishes to thank Mrs. William Mensi.

The ideas of many other authors are in this volume because the author studied under them, read their work, or learned from them because of their method in transforming what could become esoteric theology into very pastoral liturgy. Some of these include the Reverend Doctor Reginald Fuller for his commentaries in *Worship*, the team of French scholars who have produced the *Guide For The Christian Assembly*, and the editors of the biblical work, *The Jerome Biblical Commentary*. As this book is intended for pastoral use and the formation of priest celebrants and parish worship committees, the author wishes to express his sincerest thanks to the people of the parish of Saint Matthew, Hastings-on-Hudson, N. Y., the parish of Saint Joseph, Millbrook, N. Y., and the parish of the Immaculate Heart of Mary Scarsdale, N. Y., where the ideas in this book have been tried and found beneficial.

TABLE OF CONTENTS

Introduction 1

CHAPTER I:
The New Order of Mass 5

CHAPTER II:
Season of Advent 22
First Sunday of Advent 27
Second Sunday of Advent 29
Third Sunday of Advent 32
Fourth Sunday of Advent 35

CHAPTER III:
The Christmas–Epiphany Season 38
Christmas Midnight Mass 44
Christmas Mass During the Day 46
Feast of the Holy Family 49
Solemnity of Mary, Mother of God 52
Solemnity of the Epiphany 54
The Baptism of the Lord 57

CHAPTER IV:
The Lenten Season and Holy Week 61
Ash Wednesday 69
First Sunday of Lent 73
Second Sunday of Lent 76
Third Sunday of Lent 78
Fourth Sunday of Lent 81
Fifth Sunday of Lent 84
Passion Sunday 87
Easter Triduum:
Holy Thursday 91
Good Friday 95

CHAPTER V:
Season of Easter 101
Easter Vigil 104
Easter Sunday 108
Second Sunday of Easter 112
Third Sunday of Easter 114
Fourth Sunday of Easter 117
Fifth Sunday of Easter 119
Sixth Sunday of Easter 122
Solemnity of the Ascension 124
Seventh Sunday of Easter 127
Solemnity of Pentecost 129

CHAPTER VI:
Sundays in Ordinary Time 133
Second Sunday in Ordinary Time 134
Third Sunday in Ordinary Time 137
Fourth Sunday in Ordinary Time 140
Fifth Sunday in Ordinary Time 143
Sixth Sunday in Ordinary Time 145
Seventh Sunday in Ordinary Time 148
Eighth Sunday in Ordinary Time 151
Ninth Sunday in Ordinary Time 154
Tenth Sunday in Ordinary Time 156
Eleventh Sunday in Ordinary Time 159
Twelfth Sunday in Ordinary Time 162
Thirteenth Sunday in Ordinary Time 164
Fourteenth Sunday in Ordinary Time 167
Fifteenth Sunday in Ordinary Time 170
Sixteenth Sunday in Ordinary Time 172
Seventeenth Sunday in Ordinary Time 175
Eighteenth Sunday in Ordinary Time 178
Nineteenth Sunday in Ordinary Time 180
Twentieth Sunday in Ordinary Time 183
Twenty-First Sunday in Ordinary Time 186
Twenty-Second Sunday in Ordinary Time 189

Twenty-Third Sunday in Ordinary Time   192
Twenty-Fourth Sunday in Ordinary Time   194
Twenty-Fifth Sunday in Ordinary Time   197
Twenty-Sixth Sunday in Ordinary Time   200
Twenty-Seventh Sunday in Ordinary Time   203
Twenty-Eighth Sunday in Ordinary Time   205
Twenty-Ninth Sunday in Ordinary Time   208
Thirtieth Sunday in Ordinary Time   211
Thirty-First Sunday in Ordinary Time   214
Thirty-Second Sunday in Ordinary Time   217
Thirty-Third Sunday in Ordinary Time   220
Sunday After Pentecost–Trinity Sunday   223
Sunday After Trinity Sunday–Corpus Christi   225
Solemnity of Christ the King   227

INTRODUCTION

A book about liturgy is almost a contradiction in terms. For liturgy is not words, or Bible readings, bound books or revised rituals. Liturgy is action, involvement, experience, piety, prayer, and people who are engaged in these or similar actions. Liturgy books fail if they describe and define, rather than engage and invite. This book is an invitation to worship, an encouragement to do worship well, but it stops where all liturgical books should stop, at the local community which celebrates the presence of God in its midst.

By its nature liturgy has a form and formality to its frame and structure; but that form need not become formalism of the stuffy, pompous sort. Form invites interest and appreciation; formalism invites boredom and distraction.

Liturgy is not a divine teacher sent to men to define, inform, declare and bestow wisdom. It is rather about the need for evoking faith in the presence of God, initiating a people to experience who God is, and describing who the Father is by poetry, sign and symbol. In the words of McLuhan, liturgy is not a "hot," information-giving and knowledge-imparting medium; it is rather a "cool" engagement of the believer with his God.

Liturgy involves words and the sacred word, but it need not become an endless string of wordy digressions. Far more than words, liturgy is about involvement, engagement in gestures, symbolic actions, and body expression. In the liturgy there is to be reverence and awe but not of the unintelligible, "mysterious" sort. Rather homage, and praise paid to God should itself inspire true piety and respect for God as a mystery. "Power, riches, wisdom, strength, honor, glory and blessing" (Rev. 5:12) belong to our God, not because we do not know him, but because he made himself known to us, through Jesus, the Christ, and it is through this Son that we make our faith and trust known to him.

Liturgy is about signs and symbols, but the sort which can never be fully explained and whose meaning can never be totally exhausted. We use bread, wine, water, lights, incense, oil, vesture, art and sacred places, none of which can be so understood as to allow for no deeper meaning and appreciation.

Liturgy is piety and prayer, not a thought-producing discourse. It is silence and listening as well as speaking and preaching, and whether of the Trappist or the Quaker type, silence is essential for the appreciation and engagement of the believer in his act of praise.

Liturgy is the expression of the whole man; not merely the external expression of faith, but the inward expression as well. The tired distinctions of inward-outward, private-public, interior and exterior are no longer valid for we are persons whose prayer must permeate liturgical actions and involve our total being.

Liturgy is a community celebration. Fundamentally, it is the piety of a people who continually stand in need of the redemption of the Lamb of God. It is the expression in faith of the people who believe that Jesus is Lord, a people who need to struggle to make a renewed act of faith in the Christ. It is a gathering of a community of persons who must ever work at breaking down the barriers that divide faceless congregations and need to build up their common bonds in faith and love as the pilgrim Church on earth.

PLAN OF THIS BOOK

The purpose of this book is to give the celebrant as well as the parish committee on the liturgy some orientation on the following:

1. The changes in liturgical practice that have come about as a result of Vatican II.
2. Ways to use most effectively the numerous options that are offered by the new Sacramentary and Lectionary.
3. Meaning and scope of the various liturgical seasons.

The revised liturgy provides that the celebrant may make explanatory comments, introductions to the various prayers and readings, invitations to prayer, and so on, as indicated in the General Instruction of the Roman Missal, number 11:

"As president of the congregation, the priest gives instructions and words of introduction and conclusion that are indicated within the rite, proclaims the word of God, and gives the final blessing. He may also introduce the Mass of the day (before the celebration begins), the liturgy of the word (before the readings), and the eucharistic prayer (before the preface); he may make concluding comments before the dismissal."

This book gives a suggested wording for such comments and introductions for the Masses of the Sundays and certain solemnities of the year.

It must be noted, however, that these wordings are merely *suggestions*, and are not to be followed *verbatim*. Instead, they should serve as guidelines for the celebrant so that he may adapt his words to the needs of the congregation, and the occasion of the celebration.

Each Sunday's liturgy is first treated in a biblical and theological frame of reference. Then, the readings and prayers of the Mass of the day are considered in relation to one or more themes that are expressive of the spirit of the day's liturgy. Finally, there is given a suggested wording for introductions, conclusions, and pastoral comments, as explained above.

It is the author's hope that this book may open up new vistas of prayer and reflection so that all the people of God may experience more fully the Lord's presence in the eucharistic celebration as reflected in that psalm of praise *Psalm 95*:

> For the Lord is a great God
>   and a great king above all gods;
> In his hands are the depths of the earth,

and the tops of the mountains are his.
His is the sea, for he has made it,
   and the dry land which his hands have formed.
Come let us bow down in worship!   *Psalm 95, 2-6*

CHAPTER I
THE NEW ORDER OF MASS: RESTORATION IN SEARCH OF RENEWAL

The publication of the General Instruction of the Roman Missal together with the new order of Mass in 1969 ushered in a new era of eucharistic and sacramental practice in the Church. The pastoral tone and import in the document ends an emphasis in eucharistic worship which was rubrical, or *direction-oriented*. The new Instruction is profoundly theological and pastoral in tone, and is the result of much historical, liturgical and theological investigation. The obvious and welcomed emphasis on the proclamation of the word of God with a new Lectionary system, the inclusion of an Old Testament lesson as part of the Sunday readings, the necessity of preaching a homily on all Sundays and feasts, a strong encouragement of preaching at daily eucharist, and clear directions that these should be biblically based and nourished, are most important liturgical advances. The participation of the congregation at the eucharist is emphasized; the laity is no longer relegated to the role of passive spectator. The active involvement of many people in the celebration, each according to his role, is strongly underscored in the revised Order of Mass. The roles of bishop, presbyter, deacon, acolyte, lector, cantor, artist, usher, are all given due treatment and prominence so that together all may contribute to an effective celebration.

The Instruction states again and again that the eucharist is hierarchically structured, with everyone contributing to the whole celebration. Co-operation is the key to an understanding of this "hierarchy" where dignity and rank are subservient to the good of all and the service each can render to the rest of the assembly.

The celebrant "presides" at the eucharist, but does not usurp other functions. He presides over the entrance and the opening prayer, presides over the liturgy of the word, gives the homily, and proclaims the eucharist prayer in the name of the assembled community. The celebrant facilitates the celebration, he does not dominate it.

The very terminology for the eucharist in the new Instruction clearly emphasizes the participation of the assembly, not the solemnity of form, for the terms "solemn high mass," "high mass," "low mass," are nowhere present in the Instruction. Rather the degree of solemnity comes from the diversity of the different roles and shared functions at every eucharist.

NEW ELEMENTS, ADAPTATIONS, REDEFINITIONS

The major work of the revision and editing of the new Roman Missal (or Sacramentary) was one of restoration. The purpose of the restoration was to return to the sources of the Roman liturgy and incorporate much of the richness of that tradition into the new service book. However, this restoration is not meant to be a museum piece, geared for the expert or designed to please the archivist. It is every bit a restored work that now needs to be translated and adapted to suit the needs of contemporary congregations. Besides incorporating some more traditional elements, the Sacramentary has many new elements and additions within the structure of the eucharist itself. Furthermore, the Instruction itself encourages adaptation as part of the pastoral application of the renewal designed by the editors. Finally, the restoration is important since parts of the Mass which had suffered from poor catechesis or defective theology can now be redefined and reinterpreted and suitable simplifications and adjustments made.

Celebrants are encouraged in the General Instruction (number 3) to take into account the nature and circumstances of each assembly gathered for worship and different elements of the eucharist may be selected and arranged for local circumstances (number 5). What is at stake in the Instruction is not merely the valid celebration of eucharist, but the "pastoral effectiveness" of each celebration, achieved by choosing prayers, readings, songs and using options suited to the congregation. The intelligent use of these options and proper planning of the celebration is needed for the spiritual good of the assembly (number 313).

The following elements of the eucharist have been reformed or invite adaptation and may be "exploited" for the spiritual good of the community gathered in the name of Jesus.

INTRODUCTORY RITE

The purpose of these revised elements is to reveal the presence of God in the assembly, to form a community of faith, and to prepare the assembly to hear the word of God and to offer sacrifice (number 24). The burden of these rites is to introduce, not to dominate or to overshadow in any way the proclamation of the word of God. There are three greetings and three penitential rites to choose from and some close scrutiny as to what is and is not involved in the penitential rite is necessary. The very nature of Sunday, its emphasis on the risen Christ, and traditional custom of the elimination of fasting on this day during Lent, indicates that the penitential elements of the eucharist should clearly take a second place at Sunday worship.

The rite for the blessing with holy water is distinctly preferable on Sundays and solemnities since it indicates that eucharist is a renewal of the covenant of baptism, and it cites by gesture as well as word the unity of the community with the celebrant by his mingling among the people at the sprinkling with water. Furthermore, even if the other "penitential" rites are used, the second and third with the invocations and response "Lord, have mercy" signify that the prayer is one which should emphasize the LORD in "Lord, have mercy" instead of asking forgiveness. The penitential rite is Christocentric in nature and is addressed to Christ as Savior and Lord. In the text of the Sacramentary there are seven examples of how the third penitential rite may be reworded, not one of which asks for forgiveness of sin. They speak of the Lord Jesus, his attributes, and his role as intercessor. The emphasis is on "Lord Jesus, you heal the wounds of sin," rather than a reworked formula such as "we ask forgiveness for the times we spoke ill of others." The very terminology in the Sacramentary, calling these statements "invocations," denotes this nuance of invoking the Lord, rather than stating motives for seeking pardon.

The collect or opening prayer which follows the Glory to God, proclaimed on most Sundays, brings the introductory rites to a close. The use of silence at this part of the eucharist is important for common reflection, and common silent prayer should be encouraged as part of the worship of the community. There should be silence after the statement of the introduction of the day's liturgy as well as after the "Let us pray" of the opening prayer. On Sundays two prayers are presented for the opening prayer, one of which is a literal translation and the other a freer composition, and the celebrant may choose which is more suitable in a given situation.

LITURGY

The Instruction (number 11) states that the readings for the celebration may be preceded by "words of introduction." Such explanations or comments may be given prior to the readings, before the preface, and before the dismissal. The purpose of these is to help orient the attention of the community to the particular rite being celebrated, and to assist the community in linking the celebration with their own lives. However, if the celebrant chooses to make such introductions he should be brief, since all invitations to prayer and such adaptations are to be short and clear and not mini-homilies.

The introduction to the readings can serve to focus them upon a single theme for the Mass of the day. However, these introductions are valuable only insofar as they prepare for the reading; they should not explain it away or make the reading itself seem repetitious. Further, giving too much of the historical background of the lesson, or attempting to settle the difficult questions of authorship and the time and place of the origin of the reading fails to respect the purpose of this optional comment. The introduction may indicate the particular problem which the reading addresses, or it may serve to orient the attention of the congregation. Used in the wrong way these introductions can make a catechetical lesson out of the scripture readings and distort what should encourage reflection and meditation into a medium of information and instruction. Nor should the comments before each of the readings make the homily seem unnecessary or superfluous. Especially since Vatican II, the importance of good, biblically based preaching cannot be over-estimated. In fact the Decree on the Ministry and Life of Priests of that Council states that the preaching of the word of God is one of the main tasks of the priest. Preachers are reminded to keep in mind the mystery being celebrated and the needs of the particular community whom they address.

THE HOMILY

The creative act of the word finds its necessary and essential complement in the eucharist. Therefore, one of the aspects of the homily is to link the two parts of the one liturgy and point beyond the first part of the order of worship to the sharing in the food of the table of the Lord. It is no wonder that the table of the Lord's word is made a parallel to the obvious table of his body and blood at the altar; and that the celebrant of the eucharist breaks and distributes the word of the Lord just as he breaks and distributes the bread of life with the community.

The homily is addressed to real people, at a given place and time, who must respond to the ever present challenge of that word but in their time and place. The task of the preacher is to apply the perennial validity of the word to the changing circumstances of our time and culture.

Preaching and homilies are meant to bring the challenge of the word into focus for present day congregations. In the homily, the minister takes on his task of leading men from faith to deeper levels of faith; from trust in God to a deeper commitment in what that trust means. The minister of the word is truly its servant, not ever its master, for his task is to transmit it to the assembly. There can be only one master, that is God alone whom ministers are sent to serve in a particular way, and whom we all are sent to obey. The key to what and how we are to obey comes from Scripture and sacred tradition which guide us as his people, redeemed once in the waters of baptism, but who need the continual strengthening of his body and blood for our continual conversion to his way, his truth, and his life.

GOD'S WORD AND THE LECTIONARY SYSTEM

Because of historical circumstances and theological emphasis, the presence of Christ in the word of the Scriptures has, to say the least, been obscured. The fact that the Word of the Lord created the heavens and the earth according to the Book of Genesis, that the Book of Isaiah promises that the Word of the Lord will be effective, and will accomplish what it is meant to do, and that Jesus himself commanded the wind and the sea and even evil spirits to obey his Word should be proof enough of the enduring power of that word. The Scriptures are more than thoughts about God, or reflections about his deeds; they are first and foremost his address to us, his people. They are meant to be a dialogue which causes and invites our response in faith and service. The Word is the message of God for us, addressed to us, announced to us for our formation, development, and growth. The word of God in the Scriptures is challenging and probing, continually pruning our weakened faith to cause it to grow and flourish ever more richly.

It is because of this largely undeveloped theology of the word and the almost neglect of the word in popular practice, that the Constitution on the Sacred Liturgy of the Second Vatican Council called for the reform of the liturgy of the word, that a more "representative portion of Scripture should be read over a set period of years," that a more abundant and varied series of readings be provided, and that the texts of greater importance be assigned to Sundays and feasts. The result of this desire was the publication of the Lectionary, a selection of readings for Sundays, weekdays, feasts, special sacramental celebrations, and votive Masses.

The major revision of the Sunday system of readings is that this entire cycle of readings is now over a three-year period and each Sunday, with the exception of the Easter season, has the first reading taken from the Old Testament. Two principles operate for the readings on Sundays: the principle of harmony whereby the readings reflect the same theme on a given Sunday, and the principle of a semi-continuous reading where the second reading most often does not fit with the Old Testament reading and the gospel, but rather presents an alternative theme for the day's liturgy.

The principle of harmony is applied strictly in the seasons of Advent, Lent and Easter where the gospel of the day is the key to the theme of the day and the first reading from the Old Testament, and the second reading from the New Testament are selected to reflect the same theme.

The principle of the semi-continuous readings is applied to Sundays in ordinary time, for on these days the gospel is still the key reading of the day, and the Old Testament reading is chosen to correspond to that gospel. But here the second reading is selected from an Epistle in the New Testament, and selections from that Epistle are read, section-by-section, week after week so that a single New Testament book is selected to be read over a number of weeks.

For the weekdays throughout the year the Scripture readings follow the same principle of harmony and semi-continuous reading. Special seasons have special themes and these are reflected throughout the season.

For Lent, the traditional themes of baptism, penance, and conversion are stressed; during Advent the book of the prophet Isaiah is read at the beginning of the season; and during Eastertime the book of the Acts of the Apostles and the Gospel of Saint John are read. The major difference between this cycle of readings and the Sunday cycle is that this weekday Lectionary is spread over a two-year period, with the gospel the same for both years and the first reading different for the first and second years. The result of this arrangement is the reading of the gospels over the period of a year and the readings of the other books occurring only once every two years.

Certain saints' days have their own readings, and for some of them there are a number of texts to choose from. In these cases the principles governing the Sunday and weekday Lectionary are set aside for the feast.

The last part of the Lectionary contains readings for the rituals of baptism, confirmation, marriage, holy orders, Masses for the dead, various masses for the Church, public officials, special needs and votive Masses. Priority is given to the liturgy of the word as an essential part of the eucharistic liturgy because it is an act of creation. It gives the congregation a source of common reflection, common prayer, and common challenge from the Lord. Just as at the very dawn of creation the word of the Lord took a formless mass and made it into an ordered creation, so at the liturgy of the word a disparate congregation is given form by common concern and prayer.

The challenge of the word lays bare our insecurities in faith and our lack of trust and our failure to live the Christian life. The eucharist is the act of redemption where we are brought close again to the author of life and source of our sanctification.

THE GENERAL INTERCESSIONS

The general intercessions should also draw their content from the readings of the day and the homily of the celebrant; hence these should be written under the direction of the celebrant with the assistance of some of the faithful whose prayers they are meant to be. The introduction to the petitions should be composed by the celebrant in the light of his homily and the petitions should reflect specific and local concerns as well as prayers for the universal church and major issues facing the nation or area. Since local concerns are a part of the structure of the prayer, having different people contribute suggestions for intentions is important. The wording of the petitions needs much attention since intercessions which have too many petitions, that are too wordy, or are too specific can often be difficult to understand. The suggested prayers in the Appendix to the Missal indicate that a basic structure to work from is four petitions: for the Church, needs of society, the suffering, and needs of the worshipping community. To these may be added some local petitions, but not so many as to make the prayer of the faithful too excessive to be effective. In general, too many petitions are worse than too few.

The concluding prayer is left to the composition of the celebrant and he may use this to summarize the theme of the Mass and the main point of his homily.

LITURGY OF THE EUCHARIST

The first part of the liturgy of the eucharist is the collection, bringing forward, and presentation of the gifts of the faithful for the celebration.

The use of a time of silence during the collection of the gifts, or at least some silence at the offertory can help in the prayer of the congregation and their assimilation of the readings of the day and can serve as a fitting bridge between them and the proclamation of the eucharist.

The collection of money or material gifts should take place in such a way that they can be carried in procession with the gifts of bread and wine. The reformed rites at the "offertory" help clarify the understanding that we are not offering bread and wine, or any other material thing to the Father at the eucharist; rather at the "offertory" we are presenting bread and wine to await their transformation into the body and blood of Jesus who is our perfect and only acceptable sacrifice to the Father. Too much emphasis on the "offerings" can only help preserve the almost pagan notion of cereal offerings of bread and wine to God, whereas the Christian eucharist is the offering of the one victim, Christ, to the Father for our salvation.

The reform of the prayers, which are said by the celebrant, help to clarify what is important. It is the "bread of life," not hosts of wheat, and "our spiritual drink," not cups of wine. These prayers indicate the rite of presentation. From this perspective, the place of the "presentation rite" is analogous to that of the penitential rite—to prepare for, but not overshadow in any way the rite which follows. Proper emphasis is on the proclamation of the word and the eucharistic prayer; all other rites serve as auxiliary to these.

The proclamation of the preface and the eucharistic prayer is the focus and heart of the liturgy of the eucharist. The clear, articulate proclamation of these is important; they should not merely be recited monotonously and perfunctorily. Their selection should not be arbitrary since the new Sacramentary gives some 84 prefaces for use throughout the year. The eucharistic prayer should also be selected for its relevance to the theme of a particular celebration.

An introductory comment after the prayer over the gifts and before the preface can present to the community specific motives for giving thanks and praise to the Father. Furthermore, a comment here can help to bridge and link the two rites of word and eucharist which can often seem to be two separate and distinct liturgies. Comments at different parts of the Mass can help serve to unify the entire celebration, centered about the readings of the day (General Instruction, number 8).

The Roman canon is always suitable for proclamation, especially on days when a proper Hanc Igitur or Communicantes is given. Eucharistic Prayer II is suited to weekdays and liturgies for children, the third is suited for any Sunday and may be joined with any preface, and Eucharistic Prayer IV which is to be used with its own preface, is therefore suited to any Sunday without a proper preface.

The proclamation of the preface and prayer should not be understood to be merely the "priest's part" of the Mass since the acclamations after the preface (Holy, holy, holy), the memorial acclamation and the Great Amen serve as the people's response to this action and prayer. These should be sung at every eucharist, and they take precedence over any other singing at Mass. The four-hymn structure of singing at the entrance, "offertory," communion, and conclusion of the Mass has been superseded by the most recent Instruction on music. Therefore in the planning of the eucharist, priority should be given to these acclamations during the eucharistic prayer above any other singing.

The introduction to the Our Father is selected from one of the four choices presented in the Order of Mass, and each introduction has a different aspect of the prayer as its invitation—using the words Jesus gave us, calling God our Father, forgiveness of sins, and looking for the coming of the kingdom.

In addition, the celebrant may compose another introduction which corresponds more adequately to the theme of the eucharist of the day. Since by their very nature the printed texts do not require that everyone use them in the form in which they appear in the missal, a carefully worded statement here will help link the liturgy of the word with the liturgy of the eucharist and thereby serve to underscore the fact that the two parts of the Order of Mass depend on each other and should form an integral whole.

One of the major works of restoration in the rite of Mass is the inclusion of a number of texts for the solemn blessings at the end of the eucharist, and the prayers over the people. Some twenty blessings and twenty-six prayers are provided to be chosen by the celebrant to fit the needs of the congregation and the nature of the feast or the theme of the Sunday. The blessing should be regarded as part of the rite of dismissal, and the gesture of extending his hands over the congregation by the celebrant is a sign of commissioning and sending forth. Again, as with the preface and eucharistic prayer, this should be selected carefully and not arbitrarily so that the unity of the celebration is respected and emphasized.

A REFORMED CALENDAR

A revision of the Roman Calendar in 1969 made some major adjustments in the popular piety of Catholics. The priority throughout the reform is the establishment of the proper of the season and seasonal celebrations as primary in the progress and span of the Christian year.

What is at stake throughout is the emphasis on the Paschal Mystery of Christ—"Christ has died, Christ is risen, Christ will come again"—and this Easter consciousness permeates the celebrations of the whole year. The week-end has always been and continues to be the focus of attention in the Christian year and Sunday is its climax with the celebration of the eucharist. The history of this day with its vigils, early morning services, and the celebration of the Paschal mystery at the weekly eucharist clearly points to the importance of this day. Called the Eighth Day, since creation was completed in seven days and redeemed in the resurrection of Jesus on Sunday, we await the final coming of the Lord on the eighth day to bring creation to perfection. It is called the day of the Lord as opposed to the day of rest, the sabbath, since communities use this day to gather for worship in the name of the Lord Jesus, not just to stop work. The celebration of the seasonal Sunday liturgy can only be replaced by solemnities or feasts of the

Lord since the principal celebration of our redemption is on the Lord's day.

The proper of the saints is also reformed in the Calendar in the light of local circumstances and popular piety. Many memorials of saints are optional for communities to celebrate as they see fit. The celebration of a memorial is no longer merely that it is prescribed, but that it applies to the local congregation. Individual saints, pastors, and martyrs have "optional" memorials whereas obligatory memorials are still prescribed for saints whose import is universal.

An overview of the reformed calendar reveals that the seasons of Advent-Christmas, Lent-Holy Week and Easter receive major emphasis. The former Sundays after Epiphany and after Pentecost are eliminated in favor of the term "Sundays of the year" or, as in the Sacramentary, "Sundays in ordinary time." These Sundays of the year have a special Lectionary principle governing them which allows for a more complete development of a scriptural theme should a given congregation so decide. Pentecost is now a solemnity for one day and it has no octave; the Sundays of Septuagesima, Sexagesima, and Quinquagesima have been dropped since the season of Lent, which is a season of preparation for Easter, need not have its own preparatory "season" of three Sundays.

The Sundays after Easter are now called Sundays of Easter since the whole season of fifty days, including the solemnity of the Ascension, is considered part of the total celebration of Easter. Pentecost is therefore the conclusion of the Easter season rather than a beginning of something new.

The Christian Church sees herself as the people redeemed in time but looking for the end of time; as a people situated between the first coming and the second coming of Christ; between his incarnation as a man, and his return as the Lord, God of power and might; between his resurrection-ascension and his coming in glory. We are a people who "celebrate this memorial of our redemption. We recall Christ's death, his descent among the dead, his resurrection and his ascension to your right hand," and we look forward to his coming in glory (Eucharistic Prayer IV). We are a people between the times of the Lord's historical life on earth and his coming at the end of time. It is not only to the past that we look as we celebrate these feasts and seasons; we also look forward to the time when sacraments will cease, when we will all be gathered in the Father's kingdom.

What is left for us is the "meantime," between Christ's historical life and his return, and to guide us and sustain us on our way we celebrate the table fellowship of the Lord at the eucharist. It is when "we eat this bread and drink this cup," that we proclaim the death and risen life of the Lord among us, until he comes in glory.

The purpose of the liturgical year is not that we re-do any of Christ's saving events, or that we make real again the unique historical time of his death and resurrection, but that we enter into these saving mysteries again in our own time. There is the one sacrifice of Jesus, but our celebrations allow us to enter into that sacrifice where Christ is continually interceding on our behalf. We do not do over Calvary, or the events at the empty tomb, but we rather share in them at the table of the Lord. We speak of only one sacrifice of Jesus' death and resurrection and by this once-for-all sacrifice mankind will be saved.

Pastoral planning, therefore, must be done according to seasons and phases of the Church year and not by the arbitrary division of month-by-month or some weeks at a time. The introductions to each of the liturgical seasons in the following chapters of this book are meant to provide helpful information about the nature and purpose of each season so that by proper emphasis and preparation the correct aspect of the mystery of the Lord's life and death-resurrection will be brought to light.

PLANNING A CELEBRATION

The very beginning of the Introduction to the General Instruction states that the planning of a celebration is important since it should "take into account the nature and circumstances of each assembly and is planned to bring about conscious, active and full participation of the people . . ." (number 3). The intelligent use of the options available, the consultation and cooperation of members of the congregation, and the continual assistance of a parish worship committee can be effective means of insuring the kind of participation which is envisioned in the Order of Mass. The General Instruction frequently offers options, leaving some to free choice and others to be prepared by the celebrant, but in all of these, the important key to effectiveness is that they be prepared beforehand.

Furthermore, the manner of the celebrant should be prayerful and one which invites the assembly to an experience with God. Preparation and the careful execution of the role of the celebrant is perhaps the single most effective means toward establishing a good celebration.

There can be no routine celebration any longer for the clear and obvious intent in the Order of Mass is for a well-constructed, balanced and prepared eucharist. A balance must be struck between the rigidity of former days and the variety and adaptability encouraged in the new Order. A eucharist which has so much variety and adaptability that its form and structure is disguised can be as damaging pastorally as a celebration which is anything but ritual because of rote and routine performance of the rubrics. In the revised Order of Mass, the achievement of such a balance depends on the local community and the celebrant of that congregation.

THE ARTS, VISUAL AND OTHERWISE

Creating a space and place for worship, using visuals for decor and reflection, and changing them for the seasons and feasts, can do much toward non-verbal communication and the involvement of the congregation. The service of the arts (General Instruction number 254) is invited and regional and popular diversity is respected in the order of the Mass.

The placing of church furnishings, banners, lighting, and sound should not be left to untrained personnel, for the artist's work is very much at the service of others. In the new Instruction the artist serves in a continued ministry, and not one that ends when a church building is completed. Fixity, rigidity, and sameness are no longer values to be held to. Flexibility, variation and "disposable" furnishings are important to articulate seasons and times and places. The very positioning of the celebrant's chair can and does say something of his involvement with the community; the cloths on the altar can indicate festivity since other colors than the usual white can be used. Starkness is achieved by leaving the altar bare and unadorned.

Banners have become popular and can be effective in creating an atmosphere or attitude for worship; but they can be easily misunderstood and misused. Historically, they descend from flags. They "say" something by their color and size, not by the words affixed thereto. Most recent attempts at banner-making do not respect this orientation and often are so cluttered with words and letters that the importance of their color and size is obscured. The best hangings are colorful and pictorial; not mere signposts or hymnboards. Placing the words of the memorial acclamation on a hanging destroys what it is supposed to be and makes a symbol a sign for the sake of utility. The liturgy should never appear as something dry and merely intellectual (Directory for Masses with Children, number 35), and the visual arts can help convey festivity, celebration, and significance.

Vestments, altar appointments, chalices, altar breads, candelabra, altar coverings, hangings, and music all create an attitude and a setting for worship even before a word is spoken in the assembly. The beauty, care, and importance given to these changeable artistic appointments can only help enhance the elements which are the fixed and established basic architecture of the church.

"Church decor should be noble and simple rather than sumptuous. It should reflect truth and simplicity so as to instruct the faithful and enhance the dignity of the sacred place" (G.I. number 279). The arts help establish a season, create an atmosphere, and indicate a mood, and should be selected and executed with care.

They serve to make of liturgy something more than a dry academic exercise. They give it its basis as an experience of God through sacred signs and holy symbols.

CHAPTER II
SEASON OF ADVENT

It has been a frequent homiletic device of preachers to inform congregations that "advent" means "coming" and that the season of Advent is a four-week preparation for the feast of Christmas, for the coming of the Lord on December 25th, the commemoration of the day when Christ came once in human history in innocence and infancy. Penitential practices are often stressed even to the point of paralleling Lenten observances, and the season of Advent comes to be a four-week penance before the feast of Christmas at which point all the preparation is over and done with and Christmas excitement takes over.

In reality, however, this is not the case, for the Babe cannot be unborn, and now two thousand years after his birth in Bethlehem, Jesus is still, and will remain until the end of time, Emmanuel, God with us. His presence has not come to an end, and his concern for us is no less real and evident now than it was at his incarnation. "Advent" still means "coming," but the coming we prepare for is not that of the Lord Jesus as a babe in Bethlehem. The coming we look forward to is that of the end of time—Christ will *come again*—Lord Jesus, *come* in glory. Advent is the season of waiting, of watchfulness, of hope, and expectation. The preparation is for the Lord's coming at the end of time. We await the Advent, not only of the feast of the Nativity, but primarily the day of the coming of the Lord, the God of power and might. Advent is not the season of erasing or re-doing time. It is the season when we await and prepare for his coming in glory, not merely his appearance on earth as a child.

If we charted it on a calendar, the season would be divided into two uneven parts. The first part of Advent emphasizes the coming of the Lord in glory and the second part of the season looks to the feast of the birth. This second part is from December 17th to 24th (the days of the "O" antiphons at Vespers); the first part of the season is certainly the longer part. While the second part of

Advent recalls the events which led up to the birth of Jesus when he came to share our humanity, "a man like us in all things but sin," the overriding concern of the liturgy of the season is our preparation for the coming of the Lord past, present, and to come.

We recall his coming among us in the past, his presence with us now as a redeemed community celebrating the liturgy as his memorial, and finally we recall that he will come again in the future at the end of time. It is these themes which emerge in the liturgies of the Advent Sundays.

In one sense, this season ends the Church year rather than begins it. Since it is not merely a preparation for the feast of Christmas, the seasons of Advent and Christmas together suggest probing questions to us in the present Church—not about what happened in the past, but about the present condition of our faith, our lives, and our world as we prepare for the end times. The questioning of John the Baptist and his preaching is for more than first-century congregations. Questions are asked of us, as they were of Mary, as to how willing are we to bear and live the message of Christ within our souls, in our minds and hearts. Living according to the word and command of God was no easy task for the Virgin; yet she persevered because she wanted to let God's will be done. Is this our response? Should not this be our answer as we await and prepare for the Lord's coming as our Lord and Judge at the end of time?

The liturgy of the first Sunday of Advent speaks most clearly of the day of the Lord's coming, and we must picture this not in terms of a naive innocence at a Christmas crèche, but rather as the return of the Lord at the end of time. The gospels for this Sunday tell of the coming of the Son of Man, a title which occurs again and again in the New Testament and the Advent liturgy to signify Jesus's return at the end of time as a judgment figure. Exactly when this will happen is unknown, but the signs of his coming are those of anguish and distress when the powers in the heavens will be shaken. The liturgy of the first Sunday is dominated by the awareness of this final judgment, and Advent Preface I summarizes the theme succinctly: "Now we watch for the day, hoping that the salvation promised us will be ours when Christ the Lord will come in his glory."

The liturgy of the second and third Sundays of Advent highlights the preaching and teaching of John the Baptist. John is the figure who more than any other stands as one who proclaims not a present reality but that which will be present in him who is to come. John is called the Baptizer and the preacher of the theme "Reform your lives." The baptism he administers is one of preparation for the baptism that will come with Jesus in the power of the Spirit. John stands as a self-effacing figure whose vocation was to announce the ministry of Jesus. John's vocation was to stand aside when the Lord would come as the Savior. The Baptist comes as one who points beyond his own life and career to the person of Jesus, the Just One, Emmanuel. In the second reading of the third Sunday of Advent the question of the crowd to John is our question today, "Are you he who is to come or do we look for another?" This gospel more than any other places us under the scrutiny of John's ministry as we seek to know how to prepare for the coming of Jesus. We are asked about the meaning of our lives, the meaning of history, of man, of the world, and the best preparation is an honest and complete evaluation of our Christian lives. Between the incarnation and the second coming of Jesus, are we the advent of the Lord in the world of today? Are we the bearers of the kingdom in the sense that we are examples of peace and followers of him whom we acclaim as the prince of peace? Are we the manifestation of the Just One, here, now? Do we bring about the presence of Christ now to a world divided against itself?

John indeed stands for us as the prophet summoning us to repentance, preparation, and reform of our lives now, that one day we may be counted among the elect in the kingdom of the Father. What remains uncertain in this season is not the coming of the Lamb of God, but our response to him. What is in question is our acceptance of him—our readiness and capacity to go forth to meet him. He has come in the Incarnation and will come again at the end of time. The question of John to us is whether or not Christ is present and active in us now.

The liturgy of the fourth Sunday of Advent is the clearest example of a celebration which concentrates on the feast of the Nativity, the second theme of the season. The readings reflect the humanity of Jesus and human birth of the Messiah as he was to be born the son of a virgin mother. Preface II of Advent refers to our preparation now for the celebration of Christ's birth, so that "when he comes [at the Parousia] he may find us watching in prayer, our hearts filled with wonder and praise."

Advent is indeed the season of coming. But coming not in the sense of a season which erases all that has gone before in Christian history, so we can remake the scene of the nativity of the Christ child. It is rather, a time of looking beyond what happened once in human history to the end of that history. Our reflection during this season is as much on the future and of how we make the future present now, as it is a reflection on the past. We seek not for an unborn babe and an empty crib during Advent. Rather we seek to be more prepared for him as he comes to us now in the liturgy, and in each celebration of the eucharist. Advent is that time to reawaken what it means for us to wait, to expect, to hope for, and to prepare the way for him who is to come again. And the key is our preparation now, in memory of the past and looking forward to the future. The role of the liturgy in all of this is to provide us with a meaningful horizon of expectation so that we as a community might gather as a waiting, expectant congregation seeking communion with the coming Lord.

CHURCH DECOR FOR ADVENT

Despite the elimination of the strictly penitential aspects of the season of Advent, the mood of the liturgy is still reflective, watchful, and oriented to the future coming of Christ. Purple vestments are worn and other sanctuary appointments may be added to

Season of Advent

carry out the mood of reflection and meditation. A purple cloth may be used as an altar frontal made of a basic violet and perhaps a contrasting color or two. It should be left plain with no words or slogans attached since the symbol of the altar as the symbol of Christ needs no further elaboration. Banners or hangings can also serve to highlight the mood of the season but these should match or at least contrast well with the altar frontal and should be of a size which serves, but does not dominate, the church architecture. Again, the colors and their arrangement are what convey the message, not the placing of words on them. Any or all of these help to convey an impression, an atmosphere and an attitude before the eucharist begins, that this season has special characteristics of watchfulness and hope.

The placing of an Advent wreath in the sanctuary is another useful addition to the seasonal decor, and the lighting of the appropriate candles can become part of the weekly "penitential rite" at the Sunday eucharist. The priest will greet the congregation and move to the wreath, give an introduction to the liturgy of the day and then light the candles while invoking the name of the Lord in the third form of the rite with the congregation responding "Lord, have mercy." When an Advent wreath is used for the Sundays, there should be four violet or four white candles adorning it, not three of one color and one pink. The reason for the change is to articulate an entire season with a common theme and purpose.

A more ambitious, yet nonetheless significant addition to the church, is the decoration of a Jesse tree. This is a fir or other evergreen decorated with different images and symbols of the Advent season. These can be made by children or interested groups in the parish, and some new symbols can be added weekly. The signs of the history of salvation may include the serpent and fruit for Adam and Eve, a slain lamb for Abel's death, the ark for Noah, the ladder and star for Jacob's vision, the scepter for the promise given to Judah, the tables of the Law for the promise given to Moses, the star of David for his prophecy, the hand with a burning coal for the prophecy of Isaiah, the whale for the prophet Jonah, the outline of the city of Bethlehem for the prophecy of Micah, the lamb for John's confession of faith in Jesus as Messiah, the tools of the carpentry trade for Joseph, a crown for the Blessed Virgin, and a chi-rho for Christ the Savior. These help to illustrate the prophecies and readings of the Advent season, especially the reference in the gospel of the first Sunday to Noah and the days of the flood, the mention of the root of Jesse in the first reading of the second Sunday of Advent, and the key to the gospels of the second and third Sundays of Advent with the preaching and testimony of John the Baptist. The use of the Jesse tree can help create an atmosphere of reflection during this liturgical season.

THE FIRST SUNDAY OF ADVENT

The readings of this Sunday provide the keynote for the entire season. The prophecy of Isaiah cites the coming of the Lord as a judge and that those who await his coming must live according to his ways and in his light. The perspective here is eschatological, of the end time when God will lead all nations together into one assembly. This will not happen by man's design, but by God's, according to his direction, not man's manipulation. The reading from Romans is a traditional reading for this day and stresses the nature of the season, one which speaks of the coming of the Lord "already" in history, and of his coming again "not yet" at the end time. Our conduct is to be guided by the baptism we have been privileged to receive, for from it we receive God's power to live his Gospel. We are dependent, therefore, on God's presence and grace to live our Christian lives, and not on our own, almost Pelagian, moral determination and character formation. While none of this has been accomplished as yet, the gospel reading invites us in the here and now to act as if the end were very soon, and hence to become watchful for the Lord's return. The mistake of Noah's generation should not be our own—to be oblivious that the Lord's demands are very much upon us.

The prayers of the Sacramentary reflect well the themes of the day's scripture readings. The opening prayer speaks of our will for doing good, and the reward of having done the Lord's work will be to be joined with his elect in the kingdom. The customary place for those found to be among the chosen and elect at the judgment scene is the right side of the Lord, mentioned in the translation of the prayer. The left side is the realm of those rejected because of their wicked conduct. At the time of judgment, one's status in this life will make no difference—what will count is the love and faith with which we have approached Christ and our brothers during life. The more literal translation of the opening prayer is preferable if this theme is carried through in the preacher's presentation. The alternative opening prayer serves better if the preacher chooses to dwell on the expectation, watchfulness, longing and the coming of Christ as his theme of the day.

The prescription in the text is for the use of the first Advent preface which speaks of the two comings of Christ, in humility as a man, and in glory at his return.

A proper memorial acclamation in the eucharistic prayer is either of the two which speak of proclaiming the Lord's death until he comes in glory.

The solemn blessing of the Advent season is presented as the blessing of the day and mentions both themes of Christ's incarnation and return, and our need in the in-between time to act according to his commands.

Other solemn blessings which would be appropriate substitutes are number 3 for Ordinary Time which mentions the necessity of living the faith in good works, or number 5 in Ordinary Time which speaks of discernment of what is right and good. Besides these options provided for the celebrant, some of the following suggested texts may be used at various parts of the eucharist to unify the celebration.

Guidelines for the celebrant's introduction and comments:

INTRODUCTION

My brothers and sisters, we gather on this First Sunday of Advent to celebrate the presence of the Lord in our midst and to await his final coming at the end of time. May a moment of silence now prepare us for the hearing of God's word and the reception of the sacrament of the redemption he came to bring us.

PENITENTIAL RITE

You are the Lord, the God of power and might: Lord, have mercy . . .

You are forever the Savior of the world: Christ, have mercy . . .

You will come again in glory to judge the living and the dead: Lord, have mercy . . .

BEFORE THE READINGS

(The lector may introduce the readings with one comment before all of the readings, or one before each of them. They should be composed in collaboration with the priest to reflect the theme of the homily of the Mass.)

BEFORE THE EUCHARISTIC PRAYER

As we offer our praise and thanksgiving to the Father let us realize that it is at the eucharist that we experience again and share our vision of God until he comes in glory.

SECOND SUNDAY OF ADVENT

To carry through the sanctuary decor for this second week some symbols may be added to the Jesse tree, especially since on this Sunday the second reading clearly mentions the tribe of Jesse. Two candles are lighted in the Advent wreath.

While the incarnational emphasis of Advent does not properly begin until the 17th of December, some traces in the liturgy of this

Sunday offer this as an alternate theme. The readings speak more directly of the coming of the Messiah with the messianic prophecy of Isaiah so splendidly stated in the first reading, and the gospel which deals with the ministry of John the Baptist. Most probably the lesson from Isaiah was originally intended to express the hope and expectation of the ruler of David's line and hence first served as a model for the earthly king of the period. Later on, however, the prophecy became Messianic in orientation. The genealogy from the root of Jesse and the endowment with the Spirit of the Lord make of this Messiah a link between the human and the divine. His gifts are decidedly "charismatic," with wisdom and understanding at the head of the list. His role as judge is clearly stated with justice and faithfulness, in the biblical sense of mercy and love for his people, the basis of any reckoning.

The second reading from Romans more accurately reflects the eschatological orientation of Advent since its clear message is the hope the Christian has even though Christ has yet to come again. Completion and perfection of our faith awaits those who already believe that Christ has come. The gospel message speaks of the life and work of John the Baptist.

The clear message of the gospel is that while the ministry of John is to prepare for the coming of Christ, it is not the infant Jesus for whom we need preparation. It is for the whole ministry of Christ that we prepare. The implication for the season of Advent is that we are not play-acting at Bethlehem, and basking in nostalgia and memories of serene events. Rather we need preparation for the taxing and demanding words and deeds of Jesus. He comes as the "more powerful" endowed with the Holy Spirit whose words demand much and whose example causes each of us more than a measure of reflection.

The opening prayer of the Sunday speaks of receiving Christ when he comes in glory, and the alternative opening prayer establishes waiting and watchfulness as necessary prerequisites to receiving his wisdom. Waiting is not merely a passive exercise, for the allurements and attachments of this world are to be purged to prepare the way of the Lord.

The preface of the day is the first Advent preface continuing the eschatological orientation of the season.

The prayer after communion speaks again of the wisdom of God and the things of heaven, the reception of which demands a new orientation to worldly wisdom and the things that pass away.

For the final blessing the Sacramentary prints number 1 of the prayers over the people. If the congregation is accustomed to using the new solemn blessings and the variations of either the three-fold or the single prayer, then the use of the printed text is suitable. Otherwise it would be pastorally desirable to use the same solemn blessing of the first Sunday of Advent and keep the structure of a solemn blessing intact through the whole Advent-Christmas season.

Alternatives to the prayer over the people would be the solemn blessing for Advent or the third for Ordinary Time which speaks of wisdom. Alternatives from the prayers over the people could be the second for love for one another as a suitable preparation for the Lord's coming, or the eighteenth which prays for new life and the reforming of our lives, and is a reflection of the words of John the Baptist in the gospel.

Guidelines for the celebrant's introduction and comments:

INTRODUCTION

My friends, we continue with this Sunday eucharist the season of watchfulness and expectation for the coming of the Lord in the season of Advent. The call of John the Baptist in today's gospel is addressed to us to reform our lives now because the demands of the Messiah are demands for our present age. May we ask the Lord in this eucharist for his grace and mercy to direct our conversion this Advent.

PENITENTIAL RITE

You are the Lord, the God of power and might: Lord, have mercy . . .

You are forever the Savior of the world: Christ, have mercy . . .

You will come again in glory to judge the living and the dead: Lord, have mercy . . .

BEFORE THE READINGS

(The focus of attention in the readings may be on the Incarnation as expressed in the Old Testament and the gospel reading, or may be more directly eschatological as taken from St. Paul in the second reading.)

BEFORE THE EUCHARISTIC PRAYER

As we pray this prayer of praise and thanksgiving, may we respond to the invitation of St. Paul in today's reading to join "with one heart and voice" to give glory to God.

THIRD SUNDAY OF ADVENT

Formerly called Gaudete Sunday to distinguish it from the mournful, somber Sundays of Advent, this third Sunday no longer stands in such stark contrast with the rest of the season. The penitential practices of the entire season have been dropped in favor of a season of joyful expectation rather than a time to do penance. The four Sundays of Advent now present a unity that is not broken, as previously, by one Sunday with a different theme.

While the entrance antiphon of the Mass is still "Rejoice in the Lord always" (Philippians 4:4) the rose-colored vestments are no longer worn to designate this Sunday as the color prescribed is the same violet color as for the rest of Advent. At the lighting of the Advent wreath this Sunday, three candles are lighted.

The tension between the final coming of the Lord and the mystery of the incarnation which was part of the liturgy for the second Sunday of Advent continues on this Sunday. The Old Testament and gospel readings speak of the eschatological appearance of Christ. In the book of Isaiah the return of exiles was to parallel in joy the first Exodus of this people from bondage into freedom, from slavery to liberty. The eyes of the blind will be opened, as will the ears of the deaf; the lame will walk and the tongues of the dumb will be loosed. The New Testament authors used much of this language in their own description of the healings worked by Jesus. The point in the New Testament miracles is that the power of God, at work in the Exodus and in the return of exiles mentioned in today's reading, was at work in Jesus; therefore, the miracles take on the connotation of signs of the Father's love present in Jesus.

The gospel clearly aligns itself with the Old Testament lesson since the question of John is really the question we ourselves ask. Are we looking for another Messiah; are we not satisfied in the coming of Jesus and the incarnation of God's love in the God-Man, Jesus Christ?

The alternative theme of this Sunday is taken from the second reading, the letter of James, where the coming of the Lord to which the author points is the last judgment. The second coming of the Lord needs re-emphasis and exploration and using it as the theme even in this third week could be valuable for the congregation whose immediate association of Advent has been with the birth of Jesus as the only coming of the Lord.

The opening prayer of the liturgy contains the phrase, "birthday of Christ" (for explanation see below under Christmas, p. 29), and the alternative form of the prayer might better be used in its stead so that a too realistic interpretation of the birth of Christ is avoided. Furthermore, the alternative form contains more explicit reference to hope, longing, and the return of the Lord at the end of time.

The preface for this Sunday may be either the first or second Advent preface with the use of the first still preferable because of its eschatological orientation.

The prayer after communion also has the phrase, "birthday of Christ," but it also requests for us divine help in this season of preparation, our own initiatives and our own self-determined preparation can become too easily and unjustifiably the major theme of the season.

The solemn form of the blessing for Advent is presented here and may be replaced by the third solemn blessing, or the fifth prayer over the people which speaks of rejoicing, still a theme of Advent, but not so obviously in this Sunday's liturgy.

Guidelines for the celebrant's introduction and comments:

INTRODUCTION

(Depending on the emphasis the celebrant places on the Old Testament lesson with the gospel reading or on the epistle of James, the penitential rite should reflect which theme he chooses. The following is in accord with the Old Testament and gospel readings):

My brothers and sisters, we gather on this third Sunday of Advent to reflect on the words of John the Baptist to reform our lives and prepare for the coming of the Lord. May we find in the presence of Christ in our midst at this eucharist a foretaste of his love and care for us to be completed in the kingdom of heaven.

PENITENTIAL RITE

You were born a child, yet you are the King of all: Lord, have mercy . . .

You were born a man like us in all things but sin: Christ, have mercy . . .

You came to free us from sin and death: Lord, have mercy . . .

BEFORE THE READINGS

(The commentary before the readings will depend on the preacher's emphasis on the incarnational aspect of the Sunday, or the more eschatological perspective provided in the letter of James.)

BEFORE THE PREFACE

We gather around the table of the Lord to proclaim his deeds of mercy and love. We also speak our thanks for his inviting us to share this common meal, a foretaste of the table fellowship we will enjoy in the kingdom to come.

FOURTH SUNDAY OF ADVENT

With the liturgy of this Sunday the cycle of Advent preparation comes full circle. From the beginning of the season with its orientation to the end times and the eschatological expectation of the coming Lord, to the second and third Sundays with the eschatological and incarnational comings mingled, the awaiting of the Messiah to come in the incarnation was clearly a secondary theme. The fourth Sunday is the final stage in preparation since its emphasis is on the incarnation of Jesus, born of the Virgin and conceived by the power of the Holy Spirit. The vesture is still violet and all the Advent symbols are still in evidence, with all four candles lighted on the Advent wreath; yet the mood is one of almost imminent completion and fulfillment.

The readings speak no longer of the challenge of the Baptist and the need for patience until the Second Coming. Rather each of them relates to the incarnation of God's Son. The first, from the book of Isaiah, can be understood on two levels. It relates to the historical situation in which Isaiah gives a sign to Ahaz that the Davidic dynasty will survive despite present difficulties (Cf. 2 Kings 16: 5-9). The other level deals more directly with the messianic hope to be fulfilled paradoxically in the birth of a son to a virgin mother. The reading is chosen to harmonize with the gospel in which Matthew cites the prophecy explicitly. The reading from Romans speaks of the birth of a man from the line of David according to the flesh, yet adds the dimension that the incarnation leads to redemption since this man becomes the Son of God in power by his passion, death and resurrection. The theme here of the relationship of the incarnation and the redemption is an alternate theme for the homilist.

The gospel is the Matthean account of the supernatural conception of Jesus in the womb of a virgin who assented to God's plan being worked through her. Emmanuel is born in time to be forever with his people.

The opening prayer of the liturgy expresses the theme of the Pauline reading since it speaks of the suffering, death and resurrection of Jesus as part of our reflection even though the mood is one of concentration on the incarnation. The alternative prayer, however, speaks explicitly of Mary's part in the incarnation since she placed herself at the service of God's plan. The prayer also makes mention of the watchful hope which still characterizes Advent.

The prayer over the gifts also mentions the power of the Spirit at work in Mary, and begs that this same power might sanctify the gifts of bread and wine.

The second preface of Advent is prescribed for proclamation on this last Sunday, and fittingly so since the focus of attention is on the Virgin Mother bearing the child in her womb, the ministry of John the Baptist in being Jesus's herald, and the need of waiting and watching, since the time of expectation has not yet ended.

The prayer after communion makes mention of the coming feast, yet does so in such a way that the emphasis in the prayer is not the day of the feast but on our growth in faith and love as its preparation and consequence.

The prayer over the people presents the third alternate of these prayers; yet the solemn blessing of Advent may still be used, and should be, if that model has been utilized throughout the season.

Guidelines for the celebrant's introduction and comments:

INTRODUCTION

My brothers and sisters, we gather on this last Sunday of Advent to complete our preparation for the coming of the Lord in this season. In today's readings Mary and Joseph are pictured as fulfilling God's plan since they assented to submit to God's will. May we pray at this eucharist for the strength to seek to do God's will and not our own in our daily lives.

PENITENTIAL RITE

You came to live among us as a man: Lord, have mercy . . .

You were born the Son of a Virgin Mother: Christ, have mercy . . .

Your father on earth was the just man, Joseph: Lord, have mercy . . .

BEFORE THE READINGS

(Depending on the homilist's choice, mention may be made here of the Messianic prophecy fulfilled in Mary, or the need to understand more fully the Pauline reading which links the incarnation of Jesus with the paschal mystery.)

BEFORE THE EUCHARISTIC PRAYER

(The celebrant should choose the third eucharistic prayer because of its explicit mention of the power of the Holy Spirit coming upon the gifts of bread and wine to transform them, linking it with the prayer over the gifts, as well as the activity of the Spirit to make us united as one body in Christ.)

As we offer the Father our prayer of praise and thanksgiving, may we also pray that the Spirit will come to us as it did to Mary, so that we may be able to assent to God's will and live according to his Word.

CHAPTER III
THE CHRISTMAS - EPIPHANY SEASON

The solemnity of the nativity of our Lord has become a feast of primary importance in our day, second only to the celebration of our redemption at Easter. Yet, this was not always the case. Earlier tradition cited the paschal mystery of Christ's death, resurrection and ascension as the primary event of redemption, and the liturgical commemoration of those events was the focal point of the whole Christian year. While Easter was celebrated from earliest times, and the elaboration of Easter to include Passion Sunday, Holy Thursday and Good Friday can be traced quite early in the evolution of the calendar, the celebration of the feast of the nativity can be dated as originating in the fourth century at Rome. Because of the feasts of the winter cycle in pagan societies, most especially the 25th day of December as the "Day of the revival of the Unconquered Sun," the celebration of the Christian feast was inaugurated to run counter to this culture.

The feast was not a commemoration of Jesus's birth, but rather had the deeper meaning of Jesus's inauguration of the reign of God in our midst. The birthday of Jesus as a King and the fact that he has come is not primary; what is central to the feast is an appreciation that this same Christ guides us still, that the dawn of God's reign came in Jesus and his kingdom was established with his birth. Christmas is not only a day but rather a hope in a state of life given to us now and shared among those who believe. It is a time of manifestation, of special remembering, that in Jesus the birth of a child also means that the King of all nations is forever with us; that his manifestation to earthly kings in epiphany is the showing forth of this Savior to all the world; that his baptism by John in the Jordan is the beginning of his public ministry which was the reason for his coming among us. The reign of God is now with us and the bond of God with man cannot be broken. Jesus the child is Christ the Anointed One of God, forever our mediator.

The assurance and promise of the season is not only that he was born a man like us, but also that he is forever with us as our mediator, the Lord of all. He was born once in history, but is still with us and works through us, so that the reign begun at his birth may spread and continue to expand through us in our own day. The reign of God came to us as a gift to be shared and this fragile world is the place where it is to grow and spread because of our faith and love. Christmas is not about lost innocence and infancy. It is about the incarnation and bond between God and man established once and promised to us forever.

The season of Christmas-Epiphany begins with the First Vespers of Christmas and ends with the Sunday after Epiphany, the feast of the Baptism of the Lord. Christmas retains its octave in the new calendar and is the only feast to do so other than Easter; and this octave includes within it the Sunday after Christmas, the feast of the Holy Family. January first is the Solemnity of Mary the Mother of God, and in the United States the Sunday between January 1st and 8th is the solemnity of the Epiphany.

The conclusion of the season is the Sunday following the Epiphany, now the commemoration of the baptism of Jesus. While formerly the feast of the Epiphany included in one festival the commemoration of the visit of the magi to the Christ Child, the changing of the water into wine at Cana, and the baptism of Jesus by John the Baptist, these aspects of one feast have been spread over other days in the season.

The antiphon for Vespers in the Liturgy of the Hours for Epiphany states the unity of these manifestations: "We celebrate a holy day adorned by three miracles: this day, a star led the Magi to the manger; this day, water was changed into wine at the marriage-feast; this day, Christ, for our salvation, vouchsafed to be baptized by John in the Jordan, alleluia."

What has happened in the reform of the calendar is to restore some of the Eastern Church's emphasis on the feast of the

Epiphany. Furthermore, while the Western Church celebrated the festival of Christmas on December 25th and made it the feast of the birth alone, the Eastern tradition celebrated a feast of Epiphany with maximum concern for the whole mystery of the incarnation with minimal interest in whatever day of whatever month an infant was wrapped in swaddling clothes. In the revision of the calendar both traditions are evident in the emphasis on the solemnities of Christmas, the Epiphany celebrated on a Sunday in this country, and the Baptism on the Sunday following the Epiphany.

The seasons of Advent, Christmas, and Epiphany are to be considered together in the revised calendar for the days after the Sunday commemoration of the Baptism of Jesus are regarded as the first days of the year. The overview is to see the mystery of the coming of the Lord from the first Sunday of Advent through the Baptism as a unified cycle, separated from the season of our redemption in Lent and Easter, by Sundays "in Ordinary Time," as they are called in the Sacramentary, or "Sundays of the Year" as they are called in the Lectionary. The "Sundays of the Year" resume again after the Easter season and lead up to the solemnity of Christ the King and the following Advent.

CHURCH DECOR FOR CHRISTMAS

The liturgical color prescribed for the season is white for festivity. An altar frontal can be made of white material to emphasize the mood and expression of the season as one of joy and rejoicing that the King is in our midst. Liturgical hangings for the season are also appropriate and might even use the same symbols, not words, as those used during Advent. The colors should be white with some contrasts, but the retention of the symbol of Advent in the banners will show the relationship of Advent to the rest of the Christmas-Epiphany time; the motif of prophecy-fulfillment will be obvious. Yet the fulfillment in Jesus still needs the perfection and completion of the Second Coming of the Lord, when "God will be all in all." Hence the use of the same symbols will convey fulfillment, but not completion.

A word should be said about the use of the light theme in the season. In many of the readings of the season the reference to darkness-light, as evidenced in the first reading of the midnight Mass of Christmas, "the people who walked in darkness have seen a great light" (Isaiah 9:1), is clear, and the use of candles and light for decor is an obvious choice for the season. However, the season for light to proclaim "Christ our light" is Easter with the lighting of the Easter candle at the Easter Vigil, the use of lighted candles by the entire congregation to renew their baptismal promises, and the placing of the Easter candle in a prominent place in the sanctuary as prescribed chancel decor for the whole Easter season.

The use of light as the motif for sanctuary and church decoration should not be the main emphasis of Christmas since the themes of sin and redemption, slavery and freedom, bondage and liberation, darkness and light, are primary in the Easter season and are symbolized by the use of the Easter symbol, the paschal candle.

MIDNIGHT MASS PRELUDE

The scheduling of the following service for the half hour prior to midnight Mass can be an effective means of reviewing the major themes of the season of Advent and coupling them with the eucharistic celebration. The service lasts approximately twenty-five minutes. The music selections are merely examples and may be expanded in view of the repertory of the choir and congregation. The service begins with the procession of the narrator and lector into the sanctuary, with the lighting of the candles of the Advent wreath, a light shining on the Jesse tree and the white altar frontal and Christmas hangings, while the rest of the church is kept as dark as possible until the beginning of the eucharist.

Narrator:
From the story of creation in the book of Genesis to the historical books of the Maccabees, the entire Old Testament is a story of God's dealings with his chosen people—Israel. The story is not always a happy one—in fact, it is often a story of estrangement

between the two parties. It was the universal experience of distance from God that gave rise to the account of man's fall in Genesis—and it is that same feeling that gave birth to a longing, an immense yearning for the Messiah who might annul that distance and create new life, new hope and love between God and his people. Exactly how the estrangement took place is not exactly known, but it is given poetic expression in the book of Genesis.

Lector:
A reading from the book of Genesis (chapter 3: 8-15).

Choir sings with congregation: "O Come, O Come Emmanuel."

Narrator:
The promised Messiah would be born a child and yet a king—he would bring Israel from their desolation to a new kingdom—one not made by man but given by God. Everlasting peace would be his standard, but only for a people prepared for him. It was the task of all the prophets, from Isaiah to John the Baptist, to announce his coming and to prepare the people.

Choir sings: "On Jordan's Bank."

Narrator:
The Promised One would come from the house of David and with his reign would come the overturning of all the world's values . . . His would be a reign of justice . . . but for the poor. His would be a spirit of counsel, understanding and knowledge . . . but for the afflicted.

Lector:
A reading from the book of Isaiah (chapter 11: 1-10).

Choir sings: "Lo, How a Rose e'er Blooming."

Narrator:
The birth of this king would not be glorious, and yet it would manifest the glory of God to his people . . . the people prepared

to see him. The Messiah would bring a new age and it would be announced not by men but by angels, his messengers. And their message . . . Glory to God in the highest.

Lector:
A reading from the book of Isaiah (chapter 35: 1-6, 10).

Choir and Congregation sing: "Angels We Have Heard on High."

Narrator:
In the stillness of the night, while all on earth slept, Christ the Lord was born. From the very beginning man was to learn that God's ways were different—not to be questioned . . . merely pondered . . . and never fully understood. The announcement was the task of the angels . . . but the first appearance . . . to the poor promised by Isaiah . . . in fact to shepherds, to whom this was shocking news . . . so they went to see him, to see him a child, sleeping our sleep and dreaming our dreams.

Lector:
A reading from the gospel according to Saint Luke (chapter 2: 8-16).

Choir sings: "I Wonder As I Wander."

Choir and Congregation sing: "Silent Night."

Narrator:
Christ our Savior has come; Christ is born to us. The Lord has made known his salvation. Grant, Almighty God, that we who are bathed in the new light of the incarnate Word may show forth in our deeds the light that by faith shines in our hearts.

Choir and Congregation sing:
Processional of Mass— "O Come, all Ye Faithful."

Midnight Mass begins.

CHRISTMAS MIDNIGHT MASS

The readings of the Mass at midnight indicate clearly the paradox of the celebration of Christmas. In the first reading the prophecy of the Book of Isaiah reveals in a messianic interpretation the depth of the seeming contradiction that God should become a man that man could become like God. The darkness of this world has been shattered, for a light has come among us. Yet, the King of Kings is born in poverty; the Lord of Lords' only majesty was a mere manger bed; the Wonder-Counselor had himself to grow in wisdom, age and grace; the Mighty God assumed the form of the humblest of slaves; the Son of the Everlasting Father was born the Son of a Virgin Mother; and the Prince of Peace had to live in a world divided by violence and sin.

In the reading from Titus the paradox is continued, for the incarnation does not mean that all is completed in this event and so the author juxtaposes the grace of God appearing among us in the nativity with the final and still to come appearance of Christ at his return in glory. And the gospel indicates that the heavenly messengers entrusted their divine message to the lowliest of men, even considered at times a despised lot—the shepherds in Bethlehem. This is a night of wonder, paradox, and reflection on the mystery of God's love revealed in the birth of his Son.

The opening prayer of the liturgy links up the theme of the first reading and the obvious setting of the liturgy in darkness since the night is made holy by the radiance of Jesus Christ. The alternative form of the prayer speaks of the same darkness-light theme, yet it joins it with the message of the letter to Titus about the "still to come" by using such words and phrases as: "foretaste" and awaited "fullness of his glory."

The prayer over the gifts speaks of the communion of God and man and the response of the Christian to "become more like him."

The preface for the Mass may be chosen from any of the three for

Christmas. The first links particularly well with the light and glory theme of the reading from Isaiah and the opening prayer of the Mass. The second preface poetically expresses the paradox of the readings in coupling the unseen and the seen, the eternal and the appearance of Christ in time. The third preface joins both the themes of the light shining in the darkness and the divinity and humanity of Christ our Savior.

The eucharistic prayer is the Roman Canon with the proper communicantes of Christmas.

The solemn blessing prescribed is that for the Christmas season. Two alternatives would take on the simpler form as in number 11 (Philippians 4:7) and number 14 for Ordinary Time.

Guidelines for the celebrant's introduction and comments:

INTRODUCTION

(The penitential aspects of this rite should be eliminated completely for the season of Christmas-Epiphany. The following may serve as a fitting introduction to the Gloria, sung for the first time since the feast of Christ the King).

My friends, we gather this night to celebrate the love of God for men manifested in the birth of the long-awaited Savior of the world. We come to worship and pray as a people who once walked in darkness and who this day receive Christ as our light. May a moment of silence make us aware of the miracle of God's love for us and help us realize that our response to him is found in our sincere love and service of each other.

PENITENTIAL RITE

You came to live among us as a man: Lord, have mercy . . .

You were born the Son of a Virgin Mother: Christ, have mercy . . .

You were a man like us in all things but sin: Lord, have mercy . . .

BEFORE THE READINGS

(It is questionable if any introduction is necessary for this Mass since the prelude to midnight Mass, described above, was to lead the congregation to an appreciation of the depth of the readings proclaimed at Mass).

BEFORE THE EUCHARISTIC PRAYER

The paradox of Christmas is that it is an event that has already occurred and yet remains a task to be completed in men's hearts. As we praise and glorify the Father in this eucharist for the incarnation of his Son, may we also pray that the mission begun in the life of Jesus may be completed in our lives and in our world.

BEFORE THE SIGN OF PEACE

May our signs of peace this night be signs of our dedication to work to establish the peace of Christ in our families, our communities, and our world. Let us offer each other a sign of the peace of Christ.

CHRISTMAS MASS—DURING THE DAY

The readings for the Mass on Christmas day speak more about the coming of the reign of God among us than they do of the story of the birth of Jesus. The acclamation "Your God is king" from the book of Isaiah is our acclamation of faith today since in the incarnation of the Son of God, the kingdom of God, his reign, and his rule are inaugurated in our midst. The incarnation is the inauguration of Jesus' mission; the birth of Jesus among us is the initiation of his ministry.

The reading from Hebrews speaks clearly of the ministry of Christ, the creator and redeemer, who now is seated at God's right hand in glory. The pattern of Christ's life is to be imitated in our own lives, ministering to the needs of others in this life and sharing the glory of God forever in eternity at God's right hand.

The gospel reading is the familiar Johannine prologue where verse 14 states definitively that Christ became man by taking upon himself our human condition; and that through this sharing in our humanity we come to see his glory as our Savior and Lord. The incarnation of Jesus is a true and definite sharing of our humanity; the destiny of the believer on earth is even now to share in his divinity.

The more literal translation of the opening prayer of the Mass speaks of the weakness yet glory of Jesus and should be used if the preacher will explore the implications of the gospel of John in his homily. The alternative rendering of the opening prayer speaks of the light of Christ dawning in the darkness of the world, and should be used if the preacher takes the references to "light" in the gospel readings as his main theme. However, this theme is not at all as strong in these readings and prayers as it is in the Mass at midnight.

The preface for the Mass may be chosen from among the three Christmas prefaces. The first of these speaks of the light of salvation coming in the incarnation of Jesus, yet the second preface is the best of the three choices in view of the main theme of the readings for Mass. It speaks of the unseen God appearing in our midst as one like us, and that he who existed before all the ages was incarnate in human history in our time. This is the point of John 1:14, the center of the day's gospel. The third preface might also be considered, however, since it includes the phrase "human weakness" which was utilized in the opening prayer of the liturgy and could be selected if the preacher speaks of the humanity of Jesus in the homily.

The solemn blessing is that of the Christmas season and should be used as given since the third part speaks of the Word of God becoming a man, again a Johannine theme from the beginning of the prologue.

Guidelines for the celebrant's introduction and comments:

INTRODUCTION

(As was noted for midnight Mass, any penitential elements should not be used in this liturgy. The emphasis in the introductory rites should be on the sung Gloria, which is proclaimed for the first time at Christmas since the beginning of Advent. The introduction of the Mass should state the theme of the paradox of the incarnation as viewed in the gospel of the Mass.)

My friends, we gather on this Christmas day to celebrate the paradox of our redemption. In the words of the gospel of St. John which we will hear this day, the Word became flesh in order that we might see the glory of the Father. May we who share this eucharist come to experience the glory of God revealed to us this day in the incarnation of the Son of God.

PENITENTIAL RITE

You are the Word of the Father: Lord, have mercy . . .

You are the light of the world: Christ, have mercy . . .

You are the way to eternal salvation: Lord, have mercy . . .

BEFORE THE READINGS

(Since the readings for the Mass are more poetical reflections than prose statements, the congregation should be encouraged to reflect on them as implications of the Incarnation of God's Son in our midst, rather than a recounting of the Christmas story. The composition of this introduction should bear the theme of the preacher's homily as taken from the readings.)

BEFORE THE EUCHARISTIC PRAYER

(The introduction to this prayer may be taken from the Mass at midnight since that statement reflects the paradox of St. John's Gospel as well as the paradox of the readings at midnight.)

BEFORE THE SIGN OF PEACE

(See above for the comment from the Mass at midnight.)

FEAST OF THE HOLY FAMILY

The placing of the feast of the Holy Family on the Sunday within the octave of Christmas establishes and gives sanction to some of the popular piety which was a part of the Epiphany time, specifically the Sunday in the octave of that feast. What has happened in the reformed calendar is to eliminate the Sundays after Epiphany, save for the feast of the Baptism of Jesus, and transfer the devotion to the Holy Family to the Christmas cycle. The theme of the liturgy, however, must be carefully understood so that nostalgic reminiscences of the boyhood of Jesus do not become the focal point of the celebration. The context for the celebration is the incarnation of the Son of God, and the elaboration of our imitation of him is made concrete and demanding in the family unit. In our day of wavering family values, as well as changing notions of marriage, it would be too simplistic to utilize this feast to grind an axe in the other direction. A defensive posture about our society's moral values should not become a center of attention. What is at stake is a positive statement of mutual respect, not toleration; peace and love reigning over all, not the endorsement of one group over another in society's power struggle.

The book of Sirach presents couplets in rhythmic style which speak clearly of a son's devotion to his parents. This text and the theme of the liturgy speak of the quality of the relationship, and patience as a hallmark of that relationship; it is not a literal statement of where to live and how to aid one's parents.

The exhortation of Colossians speaks of submission and love for each other, values which do need positive elaboration in our time. The context of society's consciousness of liberation may lead the preacher to make statements about liberation. Yet, domination of one class of society over another, of one color of people over another, of one sex over another is not endorsed in the Scriptures. What is endorsed is rather the liberation of us all to the Gospel of Jesus which curiously brings its own strictures and limitations. Liberation is a prime value for the Christian, provided that liberation is in terms of gospel values and spreading the word of God. The gospel of the day from St. Matthew provides more of a setting to the feast than it does historical details of what happened on the way home from Jerusalem. The context of the feast should be kept in mind, that the Father's love was and is incarnate in Jesus, and that what is at the basis of our desire to grow in love and patience is first and primarily God's love and patience which he exercises toward us. It is not that we manufacture love and kindness, but that our acts of love are responses to God's initiative to us through Jesus.

The opening prayer of the liturgy speaks of imitation of the Holy Family, and the setting of the proclamation of this prayer is the assembly of God's people who believe and trust in his love and kindness. The alternative wording speaks more directly and clearly of the nature of this feast, of the context of Christmas and the Son's dwelling in time to sanctify our earthly pilgrimage.

The prayer over the gifts speaks of imitation again, but this time in terms of Mary and Joseph. There is no special preface for this feast and this is fortunate since the celebrant is free to choose from among the Christmas prefaces, which selection links the feast with the seasonal emphasis on God's love revealed in Jesus. This is also reiterated in the selection of the Roman Canon for the eucharistic prayer and the proper communicantes for Christmas.

The prayer after communion speaks of the ideal of living in peace, but assures us as well of the grace of God needed for living up to this ideal from the eucharist we receive, which is itself a sign of the Father's concern for us.

The blessing for the day is taken from the prayers over the people and should be suitably replaced by the solemn blessing for Christmas.

Guidelines for the celebrant's introduction and comments:

INTRODUCTION

My brothers and sisters, we gather today to celebrate the feast of the Holy Family, and the readings today speak of our responsibilities toward one another at home as well as in all the areas of our lives. As we begin the celebration let us pause and ask the Lord to aid us in showing his love, mercy, and patience to others in our own families and to all who live in our troubled world.

PENITENTIAL RITE

You came to teach us the Father's will: Lord, have mercy . . .

You freely accepted death for our salvation: Christ, have mercy . . .

You remain forever as our mediator with the Father: Lord, have mercy . . .

BEFORE THE READINGS

Before the first reading. The book of Sirach is a collection of wise sayings on human behavior. This first reading is from a section of this book on a son's duty toward his parents.

Before the second reading. This second reading concerns the Christian life and how it should be led in the midst of a world with different values and standards. The main emphasis of the passage is on the vocation of the married, but its message applies equally to all the baptized.

BEFORE THE SIGN OF PEACE

May we realize the ideal of unity Christ presents to us today and see in our signs of peace signs of our dedication to work to achieve that unity in Christ. Let us offer each other a sign of peace.

SOLEMNITY OF MARY, MOTHER OF GOD

This octave day of Christmas has had a number of themes for its celebration as a Christian feast. Originally in the city of Rome this day took on great significance, especially after the Julian reform, and was a day of great festivity and rejoicing. The octave day as a secular festival preceded the theme of the Christian celebration of the circumcision of Jesus which itself was the result of a tendency to set up a biographical sequence following Christmas which commemorated Christ's birth. The feast, however, was first and foremost a Marian feast at Rome and commemorated our Lady as the Mother of God; and was the primary and only Marian feast native to Rome. Hence, the feast of the Circumcision, the octave of Christmas, and a feast of Mary are all subsumed in the reformed calendar under the title of the Solemnity of Mary, Mother of God.

The readings for the feast are comparatively brief and begin with the pronouncement of the Aaronic blessing. The reference to the "name" in the last verse requires emphasis and explanation since for the Hebrew mentality to invoke another's name was to indicate a relationship with that person. Furthermore, to "bless" means to praise, glorify, and extol someone; secondarily does it mean that a thing or person is consecrated. Therefore, we bless God during the eucharistic prayer by proclaiming the redemption he has granted us through the name of his Son, Jesus Christ.

The reading from Galatians speaks of the birth of Jesus, the Son of God, but speaks equally clearly about our status through Jesus as adopted sons of God. The relationship of the believer and his God through Christ is sonship, not slavery, and the birth of Christ is understood as an event by which men of all time may find access to the Father through his Son.

The gospel reading from Luke used on this feast speaks of the name of Jesus given to the child and the observing of the law at his circumcision, facts which are also reflected in the second reading, "born under the law."

Two major themes emerge for meditation of this feast. The first is salvation in the name of Jesus, taken from the first and gospel readings, and what it means to invoke the name of God at our worship. The second theme is that of the title of the feast, for the reading from Galatians and the gospel both speak of Mary's motherhood and her faith and trust in God's plan.

The choice of the theme for the homily will determine the choice of the opening prayer, for the more literal form is introduced with an invocation of Mary, the mother of the Lord, and the alternative rendering speaks of the name of Jesus.

The prayer over the gifts speaks of the Mother of God as does the prescribed Preface I of the Blessed Virgin Mary, and the proper communicantes of the Roman Canon for the Christmas season.

The final blessing presented for the feast is chosen from the prayers over the people and is a blessing in the name of Jesus the Lord. An appropriate alternative would be the solemn blessing of the Blessed Virgin Mary, number 15, for this prayer expresses the redemption of God through the birth of Mary's Son, or the solemn blessing for the New Year, number 3.

Guidelines for the celebrant's introduction and comments:

(The introduction should be taken from the theme of the Mass chosen by the celebrant. The introduction to the Mass should provide a focus of attention for the community.)

PENITENTIAL RITE

Lord Jesus, you are mighty God and prince of peace: Lord, have mercy . . .

Lord Jesus, you are the Son of God and Son of Mary: Christ, have mercy . . .

Lord Jesus, you are the Word made flesh and splendor of the Father: Lord, have mercy . . .

BEFORE THE READINGS

Before the first reading. Today's first reading from the Old Testament recalls the triple blessing and invocation of God's name upon the Israelites after their Temple worship. It is read for us so we might be aware that in the birth of Jesus has come the fullness of all divine blessings to mankind.

Before the second reading. This second reading describes the effects of Christ's coming, for we, his followers, are called sons of God and heirs of his kingdom. For St. Paul salvation comes from faith in Jesus and conducting ourselves as sons of God.

BEFORE THE EUCHARISTIC PRAYER

We gather around the Lord's table during this prayer to praise and bless the Father for the incarnation of his Son and to invoke his blessing upon these gifts of bread and wine that they may become the sacrifice of the Lord's body and blood.

AFTER COMMUNION

In the fullness of time God sent his Son, born of woman so that we might be adopted sons of the Father. We are no longer slaves but sons of God. And so we make our prayer in the name of Jesus to the Father.

SOLEMNITY OF THE EPIPHANY

(In the United States, the solemnity of the Epiphany is celebrated on a Sunday and replaces the liturgy of the second Sunday after Christmas).

The origin of the feast of the Epiphany is a difficult historical and liturgical problem. This day has a strong pagan background; for example, in Egypt this time of the winter solstice was celebrated as the turning of the year and a time of new beginnings. In the East, Epiphany was the feast of the Lord's baptism and manifestation as Son of God. It was an important festival for the celebration of baptisms everywhere but at Rome, for the Western tradition was to celebrate this day as the feast of the visit of the magi. The themes for the feast, according to the tradition, include the nativity of Jesus, the baptism of Christ, the commemoration of the Cana miracle, and even the transfiguration. To say the least, there is an ambiguity in the history and liturgy of this day.

The readings in the Lectionary indicate that the theme of the manifestation of Christ to all nations is the primary emphasis of the feast. The reading from chapter 60 of the book of Isaiah speaks about those who come from afar, who bring the wealth of the nations in homage, to celebrate this manifestation of the power of God. In its original context this referred to the return of the exiles to Jerusalem as patterned on the event of the Exodus. The Christian interpolation involves the emphasis on the Christ event as the manifestation of God's power and love which transcends the events of the Exodus and the exile as well. The first line of the reading about "light" is another, quite dominant theme, as expressed in the prayers and blessing of the Sacramentary. In the reading from Ephesians God's plan of salvation is revealed where all nationalities are coheirs, beginning with the abolition of any Jew-Greek dichotomy. All now share equally in the love of God for men.

The gospel is the account in Matthew of the adoration of the magi as a proper and fitting response to the incarnation. Wonder, awe, and majesty are responses of mortal men as they come face to face with God through Christ.

The opening prayers of the liturgy speak both of the revelation of the Son of God to the nations and of the Incarnation of Jesus as a light for the nations.

In the prescribed preface for the Epiphany Christ as the light of all peoples is pictured as the glory of God among us to restore our fallen humanity.

In the Roman Canon, the proper communicantes for the feast speaks of the glory of God empowering the humanity of mankind.

The light theme is part of the prayer after communion and is again made the light for our guidance as believers.

The solemn blessing for Epiphany is presented as the conclusion of the Mass and has references to the light of the world and the guidance of the star. An appropriate prayer over the people to substitute for this solemn blessing is number 7, which also speaks of the light of God's grace coming upon his people.

Guidelines for the celebrant's introduction and comments:

INTRODUCTION

We gather on this day to celebrate the solemnity of the manifestation of Christ to all peoples of the earth. At this eucharist we offer our prayer of homage, reverence, and honor to the Father through Christ, the light of the nations. May our response to the presence of God in our midst at the eucharist be filled with awe and wonder at the incarnation of the Son of God.

PENITENTIAL RITE

You are the light of all the nations: Lord, have mercy . . .

You are the Savior of all the peoples of the earth: Christ, have mercy . . .

You are our Lord and God forever: Lord, have mercy . . .

BEFORE THE READINGS

(Depending on the theme of the homily for the day, the introduction should speak of the light revealed in Christ or the revelation of God's love to all nations of the earth.)

BEFORE THE EUCHARISTIC PRAYER

Christ is revealed to us today as the salvation of all the peoples and nations of the earth. He reveals himself to us at this altar as the source of all unity and the bond of our peace. May this eucharist make us one body, one spirit in Christ.

BEFORE THE SIGN OF PEACE

May the sign of peace we make today be a sign of our dependence upon him to make the peace we seek to achieve in this world complete in his kingdom.

THE BAPTISM OF THE LORD

The celebration of the Baptism of the Lord marks the end of the Christmas-Epiphany season since the time "of the year," or ordinary time begins the following day. *(With the reformed calendar the Sundays after Epiphany and the Epiphany season have been dropped in favor of introducing the Sundays in ordinary time which continue until the Feast of Christ the King.)*

The feast is a fitting conclusion to the Christmas season since the focus of attention during this season has been the implications of the Nativity, not the retelling of the story of Bethlehem. The feast is a fitting climax to the season of expectation, the advent of the Lord, his manifestation to all the nations, and the inauguration of his ministry at his baptism.

The first reading from Deutero-Isaiah is the first of the celebrated "servant songs" of this work. The selection of this lesson is not arbitrary, for the servant songs greatly influenced the formation of the Gospel narratives about Jesus' mission, especially the initial statements about his establishing the reign of his Father. Exactly who the original "servant" was at the time of the composition of the songs is a matter of scholarly debate. What is clear is the identification of Jesus with the servant, for both the task of proclamation and action in the vision of Isaiah are part of Jesus' task.

The selection from the Acts of the Apostles is interesting since it is the only New Testament writing, except for the Gospels themselves, which speaks of the baptism of Jesus. It is a proper introduction to an understanding of Jesus' ministry since it indicates that he is anointed with the Holy Spirit, brings the good news of the Gospel to the poor, and heals those who are in the grip of the devil's power.

The gospel of St. Matthew recounts the Matthean form of the baptism of Jesus by the Baptist. There are a group of scholars who maintain that placing emphasis on the baptism of Jesus at the beginning of the Gospel of Matthew has deep theological significance, for the picture of Jesus in the gospel of Matthew is the new Moses, the giver of the new Law. As such, his legacy is a compendium in five sections, like the first five books of the Old Testament, the Torah, the Law. As in the beginning verses of the book of Genesis, where the "mighty wind" swept over the waters, the Spirit hovers over at the scene of his baptism to empower him to do the Father's work, no longer of creation but of redemption.

For the opening prayer of the liturgy there are three choices; the first speaks of our fidelity to our baptism and the call each of us has received who have been reborn in water and the Holy Spirit. The second is the customary alternative form of prayer which speaks of following Christ in fitting imitation of his service. The final is the least appealing of all since, in comparison with the other two which use the language and imagery of the feast, this speaks flatly of the humanity–divinity of Jesus.

The prescribed preface of the feast speaks of the coming of the Spirit to usher in the ministry of Jesus as seen in the gospel reading, and takes up as well the imagery of the Isaian lesson about the mission of the servant Jesus.

The prayer after communion parallels the development of the opening prayer since it views the Christian life in terms of putting into practice the words and deeds of Jesus as our response to our baptism. This is a fitting prayer after communion since it is at the eucharist that we renew our commitment to the Christian life and receive the grace and strength of God to fulfill that commitment.

The final blessing is taken from the prayers over the people and was chosen because of its obvious reference to light. An appropriate alternative to complete the use of the solemn blessings throughout the Advent-Christmas-Epiphany season is number 10 for Ordinary Time or number 12 which speaks of a living faith as our response to the eucharist.

Guidelines for the celebrant's introduction and comments:

INTRODUCTION

My friends, we gather this day to commemorate the baptism of Jesus and the beginning of his public ministry. The eucharist we celebrate is the renewal of the covenant made between God and ourselves at our own baptism and which is to continue in our lives of faith. May we who commemorate the beginning of the work of the servant Jesus seek to rededicate ourselves to doing the will of the Father.

PENITENTIAL RITE

You came to bring good news to the poor: Lord, have mercy . . .

You came to bring joy to those in darkness: Christ, have mercy . . .

You came to bring joy to those who are in sorrow: Lord, have mercy . . .

BEFORE THE READINGS

Before the first reading. To be a slave or a servant of another in our society is to assume a position of humiliation. In this reading, however, the servant of God is the exalted minister of his reign and his Word.

Before the second reading. The servant, Jesus, in the second reading is the one who perfectly fulfilled the Father's will by his preaching and life on earth.

BEFORE THE SIGN OF PEACE

May our signs of peace on this feast be signs of our willing service for each other, and those most in need of the peace of Christ. Let us offer one another a sign of his peace.

CHAPTER IV
THE LENTEN SEASON AND HOLY WEEK

It may seem strange at first to begin a section on Lent with a discussion of Holy Week as well. However, the General Instruction (number 7) clearly defines Lent as a preparation for the celebration of Easter, a time of renewal for the community to recall their baptism, and a time of reconciliation with each other before the feast of Easter. The central theme of the season is conversion; a conversion as radical as redirecting one's whole life according to the Gospel of Jesus, and as total as requiring the surrender of life, the price which the Savior had to endure for our salvation. Baptism is the initial moment of that conversion and is the sacrament of regeneration, but conversion is a process which is not completed all at once or once and for all by the celebration of the sacrament. It is rather a continual summons for the Christian, individually and as a member of a community, to re-conversion and re-defining his life as a member of the Body of Christ. The season of Lent is a preparation for a second baptism in the sacrament of penance for the already initiated, as much as it is a preparation of the uninitiated for his baptism.

EASTER LITURGY AND HOLY WEEK

For the earliest Christians, all liturgy was Easter liturgy and every act of common worship was a celebration of the presence of the risen Christ in their midst. The feast of Easter itself was not merely the celebration of the resurrection of Christ, but was rather the feast of the whole process of the redemption. There was one feast to celebrate the events of the passion, death, and resurrection of the Lord. It was termed the *Pascha*—the passage of Christ from death to life. During the first three centuries a single celebration of the Easter mystery was the custom, but even within that time there emerged a tendency to expand the feast to a three-day *triduum sacrum*. The events of the death, burial, and resurrection were then celebrated from Good Friday to Sunday morning. (The new Sacramentary now considers Holy Thursday,

Good Friday, and Holy Saturday as the Easter triduum.) In the church of Jerusalem in the fourth century this trend crystallized, for the various events of our Lord's passion were commemorated at the exact places where they had originally taken place. The ever-present tendency to historicize the events involved in the Holy Week liturgy, by presenting in a step-by-step fashion an unfolding tableau of the death of Jesus, began at this early stage in the Church's history.

The recent revisions in the Holy Week liturgy and the emergence of the new Lectionary reflect a return to the more traditional understanding of Easter whereby each celebration in Holy Week refers to the entire Easter mystery. Hence, suffering and death are not to be seen in isolation, and resurrection has more than a vague connection with the death of the Lord. The reading of the Passion is now confined to two days in Holy Week, Passion (Palm) Sunday and Good Friday. Its presence in the Passion Sunday liturgy highlights the theme of the entire week, the entire Paschal Mystery, so that this Sunday with the blessing of palm and palm processions is intrinsically connected to the whole of Holy Week; it is not just a representation of Jesus' entry into Jerusalem.

The reading of the Passion according to Saint John on Good Friday is significant because in John's theological perspective the cross is a symbol of hope, and not just the place for the suffering and death of Jesus. For John, the cross is a throne of glory, the place where the manifestation of the glory of the God-man takes place for the last time.

The crucifixion is not merely the scene of the death of Jesus; it necessarily points beyond itself to the term of the Paschal Mystery—the resurrection and glorification of Jesus. It is no longer a place of death; it is the place where death came to an end and life came to all men. The human skull often pictured at the foot of the cross in Christian art reminds us that Adam's sin, which brought the reign of sin to the world, has come to an end in sacrifice of the new Adam—Christ. But God's act of grace is out of all proportion to Adam's wrongdoing. For if the wrongdoing of that one man brought sin upon so many, its effect is vastly exceeded by the grace of God and the gift that came to so many by the grace of the one man, Jesus Christ *cf. Romans 5:15, part of the second reading, liturgy of the first Sunday of Lent.*

During Holy Week two events occurred which, by their very nature, personalized for the individual Christian the events commemorated during these days—the reception of baptism and penance. Emphasis on both of these sacraments is restored in the revised rites of Holy Week. The Easter Vigil is indeed the climactic point of the paschal celebration, and the initiation of the newly-instructed Christians into the community of believers at baptism is the high point of the service. There can be no better time to celebrate an individual's initiation into the life of the church and its faith than during the very celebration at which the whole community recalls the events which brought that life to men. Holy Saturday was the day for the baptism and Lent was the season of final preparation for this event. On the Sundays of Lent, those to be baptized came before the bishop to learn the Creed and the Our Father and to undergo the final scrutinies before baptism.

A basic theme for Lent stems from this baptismal orientation, for recalling one's own baptism and striving to adhere more closely to the demands of that baptism are fundamental to the spirit of the season. A second theme which had also emerged as basic for Lent is that of reconciliation with the community. At the beginning of Lent those who had broken full communion with the church enrolled themselves among the penitents and spent their preparation for Easter in special prayer, fasting, and religious practices so that on Holy Thursday they would be received back into the community by the bishop and hence, could partake in the paschal eucharist.

The entire season of Lent is marked by a call to live up to the obligations of one's baptism and to do penance in repentance for one's sins. Fasting and almsgiving were concrete expressions of the works of penance. While originally the fast was for one or two days prior to the *triduum sacrum*, it soon became common that people would voluntarily fast for forty days in imitation of Jesus' fast in the desert. Hence, Lent was traditionally forty days long and the extension of this preparation to the Septuagesima season only served to eclipse this time of direct preparation by providing an unnecessary "preparation for the preparation."

As the Jew of the Old Testament saw the Passover as the most significant deed worked by God for his people, and the annual celebration of this event as the focal point of the whole year, so the Christian views the Passover of Jesus as that which transcends all of the Old Law, and the days of Holy Week as the focus of the Church year. What was written in the Commentary on the *Mishnah* on the Passover can also be said of the celebration of Holy Week. We must thank, praise, adore, glorify, extol, honor, bless, exalt, and reverence God, who performed miracles for our ancestors and for us; for he brought his people from bondage to freedom; he changed sorrow into joy; mourning into a celebration. He led his people from darkness into light, and from slavery to redemption—let us therefore sing before him "Hallelujah."

THE SUNDAYS OF LENT

With the reform of the Roman calendar many of the more traditional aspects of the season of Lent have been restored. The former distinction between the first four weeks as lenten time and the last two weeks as passiontide is now eliminated. The season is now understood as a unit from Ash Wednesday through the six weeks of Lent. The fourth Sunday of Lent no longer has the semi-festive quality of the former Laetare Sunday. While the word "laetare" is still the beginning of the entrance antiphone, and rose-colored vestments may still be used, the mood of the day is the same as the rest of Lent: prayerful, reflective, in preparation for the coming feast of rejoicing and triumph at Easter. Thus, the fourth Sunday of Lent is no longer a joyful hiatus in the "penitential" liturgies of the Sundays, for instead each of them builds on the other to present a positive reorientation of the believer toward his baptism in Christ and consequent responsibilities. Furthermore, the fifth Sunday of Lent is no longer called "Passion Sunday" as this term now more appropriately describes the former "Palm Sunday" since this is the only day in Holy Week, other than Good Friday, when the Passion narrative is proclaimed.

The Sundays of Lent themselves, especially in the "A" cycle of readings, present fundamental aspects of the Christian life and applications of the sacrament of regeneration in baptism. The first Sunday contains the Matthean account of the temptation of Jesus, and the second Sunday is the account of the transfiguration of Jesus which in itself places the passion, death, and resurrection of Jesus in the perspective of the glory of his transfiguration. The third, fourth, and fifth Sundays do not have the gospel reading taken from St. Matthew, which is the custom for most Sundays in the "A" cycle. Instead, the readings are from the great Johannine discourses on new life in Christ for they include the incident of the Samaritan woman at the well, the cure of the man born blind by his washing in the pool of water, and the raising of Lazarus from the dead and the statement of Jesus that he is the resurrection and the life. The readings were carefully selected to provide the entire community ample reflection about their own baptism and about the baptism of those who will be initiated during the paschal season. The reading of the Passion according to St. Matthew is assigned to Passion Sunday in order to set the tone for the rest of Holy Week—a solemn commemoration of Jesus' death and resurrection.

In the new Sacramentary, new prefaces are assigned for each of the Sundays of Lent which speak of the gospel proclamation of the day and are to be used only on the Sunday itself. Other prefaces are assigned for the weekdays of the season.

An adjustment in the penitential rite of the Mass for the Lent-Easter time would be to utilize the optional introductory rite of the new Sacramentary which calls for the blessing and sprinkling of holy water. This would be especially proper since the readings speak so clearly about the place of water and baptism in the life of the believer and this is an opportunity to show in sign and gesture that the eucharist is the weekly renewal of the covenant first made at the font of baptism.

The Sacramentary also provides new Mass formulas for the weekdays of Lent as well as new Sunday prayers and prefaces. One difference between the former structure of the eucharist and the revision is the absence in the new Sacramentary of the prayers over the people at weekday celebrations and their introduction on Sundays instead. The Alleluia is not sung during Lent, nor is the Glory to God sung or proclaimed until special emphasis is given to each of these at the Easter Vigil celebration.

CHURCH DECOR FOR LENT

The prescribed vesture for the season is violet. An altar frontal similar to the one described for use in Advent may also be used for Lent. The use of hangings or banners which have the same colors as those in the altar frontal will also create an atmosphere attuned to the meaning of the penance and the conversion called for in this season. The use of the same hangings as those used in Advent would be inappropriate since the symbols should not be the same, as the seasons are very different in theme and theology.

The use of various forms of crosses is most appropriate for Lent, whereas symbols such as the root of Jesse, and the peaceable kingdom are appropriate for Advent. The conventional practice of covering statues and images during "Passiontide" is left to the discretion of the national episcopal conferences and the decision of the bishops of the United States is to leave them uncovered. In countries where the custom still remains, they are covered only until the beginning of the Paschal Vigil so that there is no air of drama while they are removed as was done formerly during the singing of the Glory to God of the Mass. The Sacramentary provides that, if possible, crosses are removed from the church at the time of the stripping of the altar on Holy Thursday. Otherwise, they should be covered. What should be emphasized is the starkness of the sanctuary area during Holy Week, not the addition of more color for its own sake and distraction. The mood of the season is sobriety and simplicity.

PASTORAL PLANNING FOR LENT

A successful celebration of Holy Week begins with the successful planning and execution of the season of Lent. To make the Easter Vigil the kind of baptism celebration it should be, the clergy of a parish should encourage parents whose children are born during Lent to have them initiated at that vigil. Also the revised rites of the season of Lent are tailor-made for converts to profess their faith at the Easter Vigil as well. The third, fourth, and fifth Sundays of the season also call for the "scrutinies" of those to be baptized as adults at Easter. This can be of immense pastoral value as the already initiated see in gesture and action the importance of their own recommitment to baptism during Lent.

Other annual parish celebrations can also be held during the Lent-Easter season which help convey in action the dominant themes of the time. The reception of the sacrament of penance by school children should be scheduled for the Lenten time so that their "second baptism" takes place when it should, in preparation for the celebration of the Easter mysteries. The reason the solemn reconciliation of penitents was held on Holy Thursday by the bishop of the diocese was to allow the faithful to receive the paschal communion with the rest of the community. Similarly, these penance services should be scheduled with this in mind to prepare the community for Easter.

In many parishes the introduction, or re-introduction of communal penance services is in order. Explanation of the rationale for such services and emphasis on their importance not only for the individual but for the whole community can be done effectively in conjunction with the themes of Lent. These parish celebrations should be held at the end of Lent or in the early part of

Holy Week so the obvious connection between them and the Easter celebrations is made evident.

An important part of most parish calendars for the spring is the reception of first communion. The season for the eucharist is Easter not Lent. While the major themes of the lenten season include initiation and conversion, it was during the easter season in the early Church that the practice of daily eucharistic celebrations first arose. Thus, the "interruption" of Lent with the celebration of parish first communion destroys the nature of the cycle. Such celebrations would be a severe interruption in the whole evolution and progress of Lent if carried out within this season. Besides, the family celebrations which follow such events are out of keeping with the Lenten spirit of penance and fasting.

One of the almost forgotten, or at least unpublicized, reforms of the liturgy since the Second Vatican Council is in the Liturgy of the Hours, or the Divine Office. The clear emphasis in this reform is to restore this prayer to the people and not have it remain a clerical preserve. One time when such liturgies of the word could be celebrated fittingly with proper emphasis is during Lent. The scheduling of weekly Sunday Vespers in the evening at the proper Vesper time can prove useful pastorally if well planned, publicized, and celebrated. These services also involve motion, gesture, the use of lights and incense, and preaching, as well as reading, singing, and proclamation.

The outline of the service could be an introductory verse by the celebrant, the singing of an evening or Lenten hymn, the singing or recitation of the psalms with psalm prayers by the celebrant, the reading of the word of God followed by silence, a brief homily, the incensation of the altar during the canticle of Mary, the general intercessions and the final blessing. These services could conclude with a concert of sacred music, or other suitable program, or they could even be the framework within which a series of lenten sermons would be delivered. Popular piety was nourished for years by lenten series and novena services and the introduction of the liturgy of the Hours may be a welcome substitute for these with the people, and a fitting alternative to the recent almost over-emphasis of the celebration of eucharist on any and every occasion. The Liturgy of the Hours, as envisioned by the reform, is to be as much a part of popular devotion as is the eucharist and the sacraments.

ASH WEDNESDAY

The choice of a period of forty days of penance and preparation for the feast of Easter is a deliberate imitation of Jesus' fasting in the desert for forty days and forty nights. The Sundays of Lent were never intended to be fast days. Six weeks of six days fast each week needed the supplement of four more days; hence, the season was moved backwards to a Wednesday. While the Lenten season strictly speaking runs from Ash Wednesday to Holy Thursday, the fasting continues until the Easter Vigil, hence the number forty is fulfilled by adding the paschal fast to the season of Lent.

Conventional practices such as the legal prescription of fasting, the collection of monies in "mite boxes" and mid-week lenten services curiously enough owe their origin to the basic spirit of the season: fasting to prepare ourselves or members of the community for baptism; almsgiving, since the money saved by fast was collected and given to the poor; and prayer was the natural result of the Gospel invitation of this day to pray with the right motives and reason.

While fasting is no longer bound by law some penitential practices of almsgiving and fasting should be duly emphasized especially if the parish community can agree on a cause toward which donations from parishioners can be collected.

On Ash Wednesday itself the distribution of the ashes takes place after the homily and before the prayer of the faithful. The participation of the people as envisioned by the Sacramentary is to be more than the mere act of receiving the ashes; rather, psalms and antiphons are provided to invite their participation and common prayer. The ashes themselves should be a true sign of repentance and attention to conversion during Lent. To help direct this kind of meditation, three readings are prescribed for the celebration of the eucharist. According to the new Sacramentary, ashes should be distributed only at the eucharist or a liturgy of the word which contains the prayers and readings of the day. The reason for this regulation is that the distribution of ashes, along with instruction and exhortation, prevents the rite from degenerating into a form of "superstition" where the reception of ashes is all that matters, rather than making them a sign of a personal beginning of the season of repentance.

The three stages needed for a true change of heart during Lent are repentance, conversion and reconciliation. The chief means to achieve this desired result of reconciliation is prayer, fasting and almsgiving as prescribed in the gospel reading for Ash Wednesday. The first reading of the liturgy of this day from the prophet Joel sounds the prophet's call for true repentance. The heart of the reading is an invitation to turn away from sin and we do this with the full knowledge that the mercy we ask from God will be granted since his mercy and love are everlasting.

The reading from Second Corinthians speaks of the continual need we all experience for conversion and turning to the Lord. The time for this conversion is declared to be "now," for "now" is the day of salvation. This conversion is the only proper introduction to the hoped for reconciliation with each other as a result of lenten practices.

Finally, the gospel reading from Matthew declares that it is not enough that we perform the prescribed practices of the season. It speaks more about motivation than about performance, about the spirit which prompts them, and not that the letter be fulfilled. A contemporary reiteration of the sentiments of this gospel is in T. S. Eliot's famous quotation, "The last temptation is the greatest treason; to do the right thing for the wrong reason" (from *Murder in the Cathedral*).

The new Sacramentary indicates that this liturgy begins a time of turning away from sin and turning to the Lord since the prayers speak of the struggle inherent in fighting evil, and that this is a season, not just a day, of repentance. The prayers for the blessing and distribution of ashes speak about blessing the people who receive them (the first prayer) and that they be a sign of willing preparation for the feast of Easter. The alternative form of the blessing prayer speaks of those who receive ashes, but contains no explicit reference to the reason why they are used to prepare the community for the coming feast of our redemption. This emphasis on the future commemoration is made explicit in the prayer over the gifts and the first of the seasonal prefaces for Lent which may be chosen for the feast. All four of the prefaces, however, are appropriate for they clearly reflect the readings of the day. The solemn blessing or prayer over the people is not used on Ash Wednesday, since in the new Sacramentary these are reserved for Sundays and solemnities during the year.

Guidelines for the celebrant's introduction and comments:

INTRODUCTION

My brothers and sisters, we come together today to be signed with ashes as a sign of our intention to use this season of Lent to cleanse ourselves in preparation for the coming feast of Easter. Let us now kneel in silence and acknowledge before the Lord our need of his mercy and love.

PENITENTIAL RITE

Even though the church is decorated for Lent and the signing with ashes are signs of repentance, inviting the community to assume the posture of kneeling for the penitential rite is an appropriate alternative gesture for the day.

You ate with sinners and freed them from their sins: Lord, have mercy . . .

You came to reconcile us with your Father: Christ, have mercy . . .

You invite us to become the contrite of heart: Lord, have mercy . . .

PRAYER OF THE FAITHFUL

The prophet Joel urged an oppressed people to seek God's favor by works, prayer, and fasting. Joel's declaration is read for our reflection today; in a spirit of repentance we ask the following:

1. That during this season the church, by its example of sacrifice and sharing may help relieve the sufferings of the world's poor and oppressed, we pray to the Lord . . .

2. That God will move us during this Lent to be less preoccupied with our own needs and seek to help others in their suffering, we pray to the Lord . . .

3. That each of us may use the opportunities to attend Mass and meditate on the Scriptures as central parts of our sacrifices during Lent, we pray to the Lord . . .

4. That in everything we do, we seek to understand the demand of today's gospel to perform our sacrifices privately and without pride, we pray to the Lord . . .

Father, teach us to pray and fast in such a way that we do not call attention to ourselves, but rather grow in faith, in joy, and in openness to others, through Christ, our Lord, Amen.

PRAYER OF THE FAITHFUL (Children's Liturgy)

With this Ash Wednesday, the season of Lent has begun. Easter is coming and we must begin to prepare ourselves by thinking more about the needs of others than about our own needs. And so we pray:

1. May we be faithful to the promises we have made today . . .

2. May we wish to please only God by our special efforts during Lent to be good . . .

3. May we wait with great joy for the glorious feast of Easter when Jesus rose from the dead never to suffer anymore . . .

4. May we share with others generously and sincerely . . .

We are your children, Lord. Help us to show our love for you by our good actions during Lent as you have shown us your love by your death and resurrection. We ask this through Christ, our Lord, Amen.

FIRST SUNDAY OF LENT

The gospel of the temptation of Jesus, read on this Sunday in all three cycles of the Lectionary, is the traditional reading for this day. Although the season of Lent begins on Ash Wednesday this is the first Sunday liturgy in Lent which allows for more reflection on the meaning of the season. For this reason it should be treated as a beginning and emphasis should be placed on the nature and purpose of Lent as a time of preparation for the paschal feast.

The first reading from the book of Genesis expresses in mythology and imagery the fall of man and mankind's consequent need for redemption. A myth is not necessarily a story that is untrue, despite the association of myths and falsehood in our common parlance. Rather from a religious context a myth is the recounting of a profound religious truth and insight; in today's reading the truth expounded is man's need for a savior. The completion of the mythology of this reading comes in the Easter proclamation at the Easter Vigil when the deacon proclaims that Adam's sin was a happy fault and a necessary sin, that because of him we have received redemption through Christ.

The story of the fall of man cannot merely be assigned to what happened once upon a time for the import of the lesson is that the creation and fall are continual happenings, that each of us is made in the image and likeness of God as were Adam and Eve, and that the story of their fall is the story of our own as well. Adam's story is the story of Everyman. A man-centered universe results in sin; a God-centered universe results in virtue. Man's destiny as the only one of God's creatures to bear within himself God's own Spirit requires him to acknowledge his need for and dependence on God.

The reading from Genesis sets up the reading from Romans which uses the theme of the creation of man by stating that sin entered the world through one man and that grace and redemption entered the world through the God-man. Through the first Adam, sin, death and condemnation became the heritage of humanity; through Christ, the second Adam, forgiveness, life and redemption are the heritage of the believer.

The gospel of the temptation continues the theme of evil, sin, and death and the need each of us has to choose and align himself with the goodness, virtue and life which is ours through Christ. The theme of choice between the two is a fitting introduction to the Lenten season for it is a time of cooperating with the grace and life of the second Adam.

The opening prayer of the liturgy speaks of Lent as a preparation for Easter, but the alternative form deals more completely with the imagery of the Genesis reading and of the tension between the profession of faith by a believer and the faithless age in which he lives; by making belief a living reality in an unbelieving generation.

The prayer over the gifts asks that the reception of this eucharist may change our lives; a theme that is continued in the prescribed preface of the first Sunday in Lent which reiterates the avoidance of evil and clinging to the good.

The solemn blessing of Lent speaks clearly of the imitation of Jesus' life and may be replaced by the simpler prayer over the people number 4 about avoiding evil, number 6 about cleansing our hearts, and number 15 about avoiding what is displeasing to God.

INTRODUCTION

My friends, we gather on this first Sunday of Lent to begin our common preparation for the coming feast of our redemption. By the waters of baptism we were reborn in God's image and given his salvation; in this eucharist we renew and strengthen the covenant made at baptism and reorient ourselves as his pilgrim church on earth.

RITE OF BLESSING AND SPRINKLING WITH HOLY WATER

As mentioned above the use of this alternative to the penitential rite of the Mass is an important option for the celebrant to emphasize the orientation of Lent toward a renewal of our baptismal promises on Easter.

After a pause for silence either prayer of blessing may be used for the water. The addition of salt to the water is optional and seems an unnecessary adjunct and may be eliminated at the discretion of the celebrant. After sprinkling the people, the celebrant returns to the chair to conclude the rite and to pray the opening prayer since the glory to God is not sung during Lent.

BEFORE THE READINGS

The introduction to the readings should be composed in accord with the theme of the homily. The celebrant may choose to emphasize the typology of the first and second Adam in the first and second readings; or he may wish to preach about the temptations of Jesus as our own. He may question the community as to what sustenance they hunger and thirst for, and what gods they worship other than the one God such as power, influence and money. Proper reflection during Lent may be an understanding of our need for this season to align ourselves with Christ, the second

Adam, who calls us to hunger and thirst for the sake of justice and to worship him as our only God.

SECOND SUNDAY OF LENT

Christians gather at the eucharist each week to renew and deepen their common faith in God, through the Son, in the power of the Holy Spirit. Conventional descriptions of faith usually treat it as a possession, or a gift from God; and the term "the faith" has been used to describe the Christian communion to which one belongs or the tradition to which one is aligned as opposed to other churches. Today's first reading takes all of these insights about faith and adds to them a more "existential" model where the attitude of the believer in trust and dependence on God is emphasized.

Contemporary reflections on "blind faith" and Kierkegaard's "leap in the dark" find a valid example and expression in the life of Abraham, called by God to leave his homeland and follow God's word and will alone. While faith has a logic and there are reasons to prompt a response of faith, there is also an illogic in what causes man to trust in the God he cannot see. The example of Abraham as the father of all believers is read for our instruction for his obedience and faith were a response to God's call, just as our response to the word of the Lord at the liturgy requires of us obedience and deeper trust in him.

The reading from Second Timothy takes the call of the first reading and deepens its meaning to include growth in holiness as a gift from God through Jesus for it is through him that we have life and immortality. Both holiness and faith need constant deepening and growth, and it is for this reason that the Christian joins his fellow believers at the table of the Lord.

The gospel of the second Sunday of Lent in all three cycles is the transfiguration of Jesus; in accord with the readings of the "A" cycle, this year's account is from St. Matthew. It is the transfiguration, paradoxically, which leads Jesus to his passion, death and glorious resurrection. His "exodus" from glory to glory, from transfiguration to resurrection, through his humiliation, is a constant theme in the history of Christian theology. The setting for the passion of Jesus begins with the revelation of his glory to Peter, James, and John. The response of these men to the manifestation of God's glory on the mountainside should be our response to the power and glory of the Lord revealed at the eucharist. The experience of God at the eucharist is inviting, yet distant, familiar yet filled with awe and mystery; intimate, yet marked by our need for complete re-creation at his hands, and according to his designs.

The opening prayer of the liturgy asks the Lord for his grace to open the hearts of believers to hear his word at this celebration. The alternative form of the prayer speaks more clearly of the readings and of the glory of the transfiguration, for in his light is the fullness of life and truth and our response to this revelation can only be one of dependence on his word and wonder at the vision of his glory.

The prayer over the gifts asks that the already believing Christians may be made holy by the sacrifice of Christ's body and blood; the basis of this prayer is the exhortation of Second Timothy.

The prescribed preface of the second Sunday of Lent speaks of the transfiguration but links it explicitly with Christ's suffering and humiliation prior to entering his glory at the resurrection.

The prayer after communion describes the holy mysteries being celebrated that those on earth may share even now in the life to come.

The suggested prayer over the people has no thematic connection with the rest of the prayers and readings of the day and could be replaced by using number 4 about growth in holiness and avoiding evil, number 5 about being blessed and remaining faithful to

God's love, number 6 about a change of heart, number 7 about the Father's gift of light or number 9 about belief and the gift of God's love.

A solemn blessing which could be used in place of the structure of the prayer over the people is number 5 of the Passion of the Lord.

Guidelines for the celebrants introduction and comments:

INTRODUCTION

My friends, we gather on this Second Sunday of Lent to continue our preparation in this season for the coming feast of Easter. As we ask the Lord to bless this water which we will use to recall our baptism, let us also pray that he will help us respond to his word this day by placing our faith and trust in him alone by following the example of Abraham, our father in the faith.

BEFORE THE READINGS

Depending on the circumstance and nature of the congregation two themes emerge as central points in the readings. The first is that among definitions and understandings of faith, the characteristic of an obedient trust in God and growth in the holiness which that faith brings is essential. The second theme is the transfigured glory of God in which we share at the eucharist only to be completed in the final resurrection from the dead.

BEFORE THE EUCHARISTIC PRAYER

We come to this table of God's grace at the Lord's invitation to share in the glory of the risen Christ. Let us pray that during this season of Lent our lives may reflect his glory and our faith in his presence may grow in our hearts.

THIRD SUNDAY OF LENT

In the revised rite for the initiation of adults, the third, fourth and fifth Sundays of Lent are given prominence and significance in the convert's initiation into the Church. Historically, those enrolled in the catechumenate at the beginning of Lent came before the bishop on these three Sundays for scrutinies, exorcisms, and instructions. In the new Sacramentary the title of this third Sunday indicates that the first scrutiny of the adult convert is held on this day in a public profession before the community. The readings of the day in the Lectionary were chosen to give prominence to this day for they speak of the primary intention of the Lenten season—to prepare catechumens for their initiation into the church, and to lead the baptized to a deeper appreciation of their baptism in Christ.

The first reading from the book of Exodus has been chosen to reflect the theme of the gospel of the day. It describes the passing-over of the Israelites despite their difficulties and doubts in faith. The reference to water recalls the event of Moses striking the rock; its usage can lead to many symbolic and spiritual connotations.

The responsorial psalm puts a different light on the event of the reading for it draws attention to hardening our hearts to the voice of the word of the Lord. The citing of Massah and Meriba emphasizes not the event of the flowing water but the quarreling, grumbling, and the hardness of the Israelites to the word of God.

In the second reading justification is described as the gift of God's love and the indwelling of the Holy Spirit. Christ died for godless men; while we were still sinners he made us righteous and while we were unworthy of attention, he made us worthy of adoption by the Father.

The gospel reading is taken from among the great discourses of the gospel of St. John where Jesus is described not as water but as living water, not as ordinary bread, but the bread of life, not as any vine but the only true vine, and unlike any other shepherd for he is the only one whom we can call "good." The reading today speaks of faith, regeneration, allegiance to the word of God and worship in spirit and truth. The issue at stake for the believer is how faithfully is his allegiance aligned with Jesus. How firm is a profession of faith in the word of God when the ways of the world offer so many blind alleys and immediate but superficial joys when compared with the joys that come to those who believe.

The opening prayer of the liturgy recalls that fasting, prayer, and works of mercy are essential parts of the lenten season.

The prayer over the gifts does not speak of having our sins forgiven at the eucharist, but rather of our forgiving others as the proper and required response to God's act of love for us.

In the prescribed preface for the Sunday, the gift of faith given to the woman at the well is again shared by all the baptized at the eucharist so their hearts may be filled with the fire of divine love.

The prayer after communion reflects the theme of the prayer over the gifts in speaking in terms of forgiveness.

The solemn blessing for Passion of our Lord is suggested in the Sacramentary and should be used if the scrutiny of the catechumens takes place at Mass. Other prayers over the people may be used in its place: number 6 about a complete change of heart during this season, number 10 about the people who hope for God's mercy, or number 15 about avoiding what is displeasing to the Father.

Guidelines for the celebrant's introduction and comments:

INTRODUCTION

The following is a suggested introduction to the rite of blessing and sprinkling with holy water. If adults to be initiated into the Church at the Easter Vigil are present for the scrutiny they should be formally welcomed at this time and encouraged to pursue their preparation for baptism.

My friends, by the waters of baptism we were made God's chosen people and offered salvation through Christ the Savior. We now ask the Father whom we worship this day in spirit and in truth, to bless this water which will be a sign that at the eucharist we renew the covenant of our baptism.

BEFORE THE READINGS

Before the first reading. The event recounted in today's first reading should cause each of us to reflect on the many times we have hardened our hearts and closed our minds to the demands which the word of God makes upon us.

Before the second reading. Salvation is a gift from God, yet we often act as though it were something we can earn and achieve. The apostle Paul directs our thoughts in this reading to place the emphasis on God's act of love for us in setting us right with God. Our acts of goodness are a response, not a cause, of our salvation in Christ.

The proclamation of the gospel should be the highlight of the liturgy of the word because of all the obvious baptismal and related themes. It can be read in dialogue form with different people reading the parts of Christ, the Samaritan woman, and a Narrator. The arrangement is similar to that used for the reading of the Passion on Passion Sunday and Good Friday.

BEFORE THE EUCHARIST PRAYER

As we offer our prayer of praise and homage to the Father at the eucharist, we praise him for his gift of life in creating us in his image and likeness and for life eternal by dying and rising for our salvation.

FOURTH SUNDAY OF LENT

This Sunday was formerly called "Laetare Sunday" since its mood and theme was one of hope and rejoicing that Easter was near. In the reformed calendar this Sunday is not different from the other Sundays of Lent even though the entrance antiphon for the day still begins with the Latin word "laetare." The day is important because it is the day of the second scrutiny in preparation for the baptism of adults at the Easter Vigil. The first reading from First Samuel contains, at best, oblique references to the other two readings. The anointing of David as king may be a reference to the anointing in the responsorial psalm both of which may refer to Christ the good shepherd. The figure of David may also be a prefigurement of the anointing to Messiahship of Jesus for his mission. Whatever the reason for its selection for this day, the theme of the liturgy is better reflected in the other two readings for they present implications and applications of the baptism of the believer.

The reading from Ephesians is particularly significant because throughout the season of Lent the community has been urged to cast aside deeds of darkness and walk in the brilliance of the light of Christ. In this reading, for the first time during Lent, the darkness-light theme which will be so predominant at Easter is enunciated. The believer must leave the deeds of darkness and live according to the justice and truth of God through the light of Christ. The selection of this reading for the Sunday liturgy of the second scrutiny emphasizes clearly that the preparation of a person coming to the faith is one of moral formation as well as information about the faith. The preparation of adults to be baptized has more to do with choices and deeds than it does with dogmatic teaching.

The gospel reading dominates the liturgy by the length of the reading and its significance. The miracle story of healing the man born blind is amplified in typical Johannine style by references and explanations about light, water, and Jesus' origins. The reference to Christ as the light of the world and to the symbolism of water as new birth is clear, for in his death and resurrection the sightless see eternal truths, and the "seeing" become blind because their former sight according to the vision of the world is now changed to the vision of Christ.

The discussion about Jesus' origins is a typical Johannine approach: if we know his parents, why can't we keep him under control? The point of the author is that if we ask this question we do not know his true origins at all for he is from above and to follow him where he goes requires a new birth for the believer.

The theme of light pervades the liturgy of the word; a light that is not a possession to be contained, but a gift which clarifies and illuminates the things of this world so that we do not rely upon human powers for our salvation, but acknowledge the divine origins of our Savior.

The opening prayer of the liturgy presents the community as waiting eagerly for the feast of Easter, hence placing the lenten season within the frame of preparation for Easter. The alternative wording, however, is a direct imitation of the Gospel of St. John for Jesus is the Word who comes into the sinful world to lead all men to his light.

The Johannine terminology continues in the prayer over the gifts as the Word is pictured in conflict with the world.

The prescribed preface of the Sunday is of the man born blind, and describes Jesus as the Lord who came to be a light for the darkness of this world. Also in the preface, the imagery of the first Sunday of Lent about the fall of Adam is continued with a reference to his fall, his consequent need for salvation, and that this Savior will come to us again as our light at the Easter Vigil.

The prayer after communion speaks about enlightenment of all who come into the world, who are given direction, and shown the way by the light of the Gospel.

The suggested prayer over the people is better replaced by number 7 which speaks explicitly about the coming of the light of Christ upon the family of the Church.

The appropriate solemn blessing for the Mass would be number 5 of the Passion of Our Lord.

Guidelines for the celebrant's introduction and comments:

INTRODUCTION

Again this introduction should be addressed to the adults to be initiated at the Easter Vigil as well as to the rest of the community who will renew their promises of baptism at Easter. The rite of blessing and sprinkling with holy water should be used on this day.

My friends, the church presents for us the annual observance of Lent so that by prayer, fasting, and works of charity we may prepare for the feast of Easter. In today's gospel Jesus cures the man born blind and restores his sight by the water in the pool of Siloam. May we who are blessed by this water renew the vows of our own baptism and rededicate ourselves to live as a people illumined by the light of Christ.

BEFORE THE READINGS

The Christian life is a response to God's call to live according to his light. The readings today clarify for us what it means to walk as "children of the light," and thus our moral decisions must be in conformity with the Word of the Lord who has called us out of darkness to share his redemptive light.

FIFTH SUNDAY OF LENT

This Sunday marks the third Sunday of the scrutinies for the preparation of adult converts, and the final Sunday of Lent before the beginning of Holy Week. The liturgy of the word of this day speaks of re-creation, resurrection, and new life.

The selection from the Old Testament prophet Ezekiel is taken from the chapter about pouring forth the Spirit upon the "dry bones" in the valley of his vision. The prophet speaks of restoration through an act of God through the Spirit and that it was through him that the people first were saved from their oppression in Egypt, and by his power they will be saved again and restored as the people of God. The symbolic meaning of the reading is the resurrection of the people to new life, a theme clearly reiterated in succeeding apocalyptic literature and finally present in the death and resurrection of Jesus.

The reading from Romans states that through Christ the whole person of the believer is saved, raised up, and redeemed. The realm of the flesh is the realm to be left behind, and the realm of the Spirit is where true life is to be found. But there is no hellenistic dichotomy here between flesh and spirit since the believer lives with the Spirit of God enfleshed in his body so that his whole person will live in conformity with that Spirit. The indwelling of the Spirit refers to the baptism of the person and his consequent moral life.

The gospel reading brings to a climax the Johannine discourses of the third, fourth, and fifth Sundays of Lent—the accounts of the Samaritan woman, the man born blind, and the raising of Lazarus. As in the previous discourses, the deeper level of meaning lies in the additions to the narrative by the sacred author and these should be explored completely. The narration of the story gives way to the statement of Jesus that "I am the resurrection and the life" and that belief is necessary if a person wishes to save his life.

The scandal of the cross is that he who is the resurrection and the life first had to suffer and die before men could live, for only by dying could he then be raised to new life with the Father. In baptism the believer dies to his former self and former way of life, and rises to the newness of life in Christ Jesus.

The opening prayer of the liturgy speaks of the salvation Christ offers us because he died for men, and uses typical Johannine imagery. The alternate form of the prayer speaks specifically of the necessity of Jesus' death and suffering to bring new life to believers who then must work in the world to transform and restore it.

The prayer over the gifts speaks of the forgiveness of sins as part of the cleansing offered at the eucharist and that those who are enlightened by the Christian faith may be governed by the light of Christ.

The prescribed preface describes Jesus the man, who wept for his friend, Lazarus, and Jesus the mediator of God's grace, who raised his friend and restored him to life. The sacraments are means whereby we, the community of believers, receive in our day the same gift of life from Christ.

The prayer after communion describes the body and blood of Christ shared at the eucharist as the bond of unity between the church and her Lord and Savior.

For the prayer over the people, number 18 about rebirth and new life is more appropriate than the one given in the Sacramentary for today's Mass. Also preferable is number 17 about the necessity of suffering leading to glory, and number 23 about the community remaining close to Jesus in prayer and in love for each other.

Guidelines for the celebrant's introduction and comments:

INTRODUCTION

My friends, we come together on this fifth Sunday of Lent to receive the strength of the risen Lord to help us live according to his word, aided by his Holy Spirit. As we bless this water we recall that at baptism we died with Christ and rose to share new life in him. May that new life strengthen and renew us at this celebration of the eucharist.

BEFORE THE READINGS

A person who is led by the vision of God understands that the prophecy of Ezechiel and the experience of Paul in the coming and the power of the Spirit has been fulfilled in his life because the Spirit of God dwells in him. The readings of today's liturgy of the word remind us that life according to the Spirit of God was begun for us at baptism and will come to completion in the Father's kingdom.

BEFORE THE EUCHARISTIC PRAYER

May we who gather around the Lord's table this day offer our praise and thanks to the Father for the gift of the resurrected life we share through his Son and our Savior, Jesus Christ.

PASSION SUNDAY

It should be recalled that the celebration of the events of Holy Week form a closely knit unity and no one aspect should be understood apart from the others. The liturgy of Passion Sunday is a perfect example of this since the triumphal entry of Jesus into Jerusalem is only a subsidiary theme in the celebration, and the passion of the Lord is the major theme of the day. The obvious drama and acclamation of Jesus as king is not allowed to dominate the major emphasis of the day for as soon as the procession enters the church, the mood of the liturgy changes from acclamation to solemn and sober reflection on the passion and death of Jesus.

The reading of the gospel account in Matthew 21 of the triumphal entry into Jerusalem is used at the time of the blessing of the palm branches, but the readings of the eucharist are about obedience, suffering, and the passion.

The first reading of the eucharist is from the third servant song of Deutero-Isaiah and clearly shows that the servant of Yahveh is obedient, and totally submissive to the Father's will. The only recourse for him in his humiliation and trial is to cry out to the Lord, his only hope.

The second reading of the day is from the Christ hymn of Philippians, chapter 2, and again the voluntary surrender of the status Jesus had as the eternal Son of the Father is emphasized since he willingly took on the form of a slave to become obedient to the Father even to death on a cross.

The gospel proclamation is the Passion according to St. Matthew, a narrative which indicates the royalty of this Savior, and which at the same time, indicates his humiliation as well.

The prayers of the Sacramentary reflect very well the nature and theme of the day for the opening prayer is a keynote for the whole of Holy Week. It declares that Jesus is a model of humility and our imitation of him as Savior and Lord must necessarily include imitation of his humiliation and suffering. The alternate form of the prayer speaks more clearly of the obedience of the servant Jesus from the reading of Philippians, and also includes the theme of the letter to the Romans for one man justifies all men by his one sacrifice. The alternate form is not as clear on the motif of suffering as is the more literal translation, but may be selected if the celebrant emphasizes in his homily the obedience of Jesus in doing the Father's will.

The prayer over the gifts speaks of the unity of Christ's sacrifice in the eucharist and maintains clearly that what we offer at the eucharist is not bread and wine but the one sacrifice acceptable to the Father, the sacrifice of Jesus the Savior.

The prescribed preface for Passion Sunday juxtaposes in fine poetic style the theme of Holy Week for the sinless one gave himself for sinners, the innocent one redeemed the guilty, and the dying and rising of Jesus enables us to share in his eternal life here on earth. Because of the almost word-for-word similarity between the preface and the second memorial acclamation, this acclamation should be used during the eucharistic prayer after the narrative of the Lord's Supper.

The prayer after communion reinforces the theme of the other prayers of the liturgy because it speaks directly of the death and resurrection of Jesus.

The form of the solemn blessing is resumed with the liturgy of Passion Sunday and should be used on such a solemn day. The suggested blessing speaks in its three parts of the humility of Jesus in his willing service of others, his death on the cross, and the resurrection to which we are all called. The theme of the entire week is presented as a unity of events and as a single sacrifice of Christ.

PASTORAL PLANNING

The celebration of the Lord's entry into Jerusalem with the distribution and blessing of palm branches is prescribed for every celebration of the liturgy on Passion Sunday. Some form of the procession is required, even if the rites for the solemn or simple entrance are used. The procession should begin in some place other than the church itself. It may begin in a church hall, school auditorium or in an open place sufficiently removed from the church to allow for a procession into the church.

The assistance of ushers to direct people from the church to the place of meeting is very important, since it will help the community assemble in such a way that all can see and hear the celebrant's prayers, blessing and homily.

The use of a microphone system in this place of gathering is a necessity for, depending on the nature of the place and size of the congregation, the sound can often be lost, especially if the gathering is not indoors.

The choir should not be gathered in a single spot for this introduction since the singing will then be isolated in one place as well. They should mingle with the rest of the congregation.

The celebrant should not be vested in a chasuble, but should wear a cope, a more fitting vestment for procession.

The distribution of palms takes place as the people assemble and the blessing takes place while they hold them in their hands. The outline for this part of the liturgy is as follows: a song during which the assembly gathers, an introduction (either from the Sacramentary, or one composed for the local community), the prayer and blessing of palms with water, the proclamation of the gospel, homily, and invitation to procession. The homily should quite properly be given at this point in the liturgy since it gives the celebrant an opportunity to introduce the celebration of the events of Holy Week. Furthermore the liturgy of Passion Sunday itself provides for the juxtaposition of glory and suffering, exaltation and humiliation, resurrection and passion and death. These are the themes of the week and should be interpreted as the themes of this Sunday as well.

At the time of the procession the directions in the Sacramentary indicate that a minister carrying a suitably decorated cross begins the procession to the church. The carrying of a processional banner at the head of the procession as well as the carrying of other hangings and decorations for the church for Holy Week may be a suitable adaptation in the liturgy. Carrying banners with the symbols of Holy Week helps to create an atmosphere of meditation on the entire paschal mystery as the theme of the day rather than isolating in sign and symbol the first triumphal entry of Jesus into Jerusalem. One specific suggestion would be to carry a banner containing a cross, the background in violet and the cross itself in green. This would indicate in the form of a suitable sign the use of violet for penance and recollection, green the color of hope, and that our hope comes from the wood of the Cross.

The color of the vestments of the day is red for royalty, instead of violet for penance, and the celebrant changes from the red cope to the chasuble as he enters the sanctuary for the liturgy of the word.

The penitential rite is eliminated after the procession, since the prior ceremony takes its place; the celebrant invites the community to prayerful reflection on the readings of the day by immediately praying the opening prayer.

The Passion is read at all Masses and can be done effectively with three lecterns in the sanctuary with two lay readers and the priest proclaiming the major parts and the congregation invited to join in the parts reserved to the "crowd." This form of proclamation should also be utilized for the Passion reading on Good Friday.

EASTER TRIDUUM

HOLY THURSDAY

In the history and evolution of the days of Holy Week, the term *triduum sacrum* originally refers to Good Friday, Holy Saturday, and Easter Sunday. Holy Thursday was in a different position because it was a day for the solemn reconciliation of penitents, the blessing of oils to be used for sacraments at the Easter Vigil, and an evening of vigils in preparation for the celebration of Good Friday with its emphasis on the cross of Christ.

As early as the fourth century communities gathered for all-night vigils of common prayer and reflection on the significance of the passion of Jesus. The reconciliation of penitents was held in place of the liturgy of the word. Since baptism was regarded as the initiation of the believer into the eucharistic assembly, the reconciliation of penitents as a second baptism was done on Holy Thursday and the community could partake of the paschal communion.

In the present reform of the rites of Holy Week, the evening Mass of the Lord's Supper on Holy Thursday is the beginning of the *triduum sacrum*, and the restoration of the chrism Mass on Holy Thursday morning in the cathedral church of the bishop of the diocese is considered still part of the season of Lent. According to the directions in the Sacramentary, no Masses without a congregation are permitted on Holy Thursday, and the only celebration of the day in a parish is the single celebration in the evening.

Another Mass may be *permitted*, but in no way is it encouraged in the directives. All should be present for the evening celebration, and all the clergy of the parish should exercise their ministry by concelebrating the eucharist.

The title for the celebration is "Evening Mass of the Lord's Supper" but this should be expanded so that the title also indicates the service theme which is strongly emphasized in the readings and prayers of the eucharist. The liturgy commemorates the last supper Jesus celebrated with his disciples, and two major themes dominate the celebration. It was during this meal that Jesus instituted the eucharist by inviting his disciples to "Do this in remembrance of me."

At that last supper, Jesus also gave the command to serve the needs of our fellow man as he humbled himself to wash the feet of his disciples. While there is only a ritual commemoration of the washing of the feet of the disciples on this evening, there should always be a significant connection between prayer at the eucharist and the service we offer our brothers when the eucharist has ended. A commemoration of this humble service, and the service we are required to give should always be at the heart of our prayer at the eucharist. We gather at the eucharist as a community of fellowship in the name of the Lord Jesus, and as members of that community we are to wash the feet of others by answering and serving their needs. We do not live in isolation, nor do we celebrate the eucharist in isolation. For, in the words of one of the Fathers of the early church, "If we live alone, whose feet will we wash?"

Besides the washing of the feet of twelve parishioners, the planning of the liturgy could also include adapting part of the Chrism Mass which is a new ceremony called "Renewal of Commitment to Priestly Service." In the revised rites of all the sacraments the conferral of the sacrament takes place following the liturgy of the word and before the general intercessions. In conscious imitation of this structure the renewal of commitment to priestly service should take place following the homily and should be given concrete expression in the washing of the feet following it. The rite as described for the Chrism Mass can be used almost word for word, introducing the word "pastor" where bishop is prescribed. The concelebrants should stand for this rite and answer the questions of the pastor who celebrates the eucharist this evening; for it is he who should wash the feet of the parishoners, lead his fellow priests in the commitment renewal, and be the celebrant of the Lord's Supper.

The liturgy of the word this evening begins with the commemoration of the Passover meal as a foretaste of the eucharistic meal we now commemorate. The second reading is the Pauline account of the institution of the Lord's Supper, and the gospel is from St. John describing the washing of the feet and the service which Christians are to offer each other.

The prescription in the new Sacramentary is that the homily this evening should explore the principal mysteries commemorated in the Mass: the institution of the eucharist, the institution of the priesthood, and the Christ's command of love and concern for each other.

The opening prayer of the liturgy describes this eucharist as memorial of the institution of the eucharist, the prayer over the gifts speaks of the eucharist as a continual memorial of our redemption, the preface for the celebration is that of the holy eucharist, and the Roman Canon is proclaimed with the proper communicantes for Holy Thursday.

After the prayer after communion, there is a procession to the repository. The community is encouraged to remain after the service for adoration of the sacrament at the repository until midnight. According to the directives of the Missal, all-night adoration and adoration on Good Friday morning are eliminated.

The days of Good Friday and Holy Saturday are days without public reservation and adoration of the Sacrament. The purpose of this reform is to shift the emphasis in popular piety away from the adoration without proper and complete emphasis on the celebration of the liturgy. After midnight the eucharist should fittingly be removed to another place until it is needed for the Good Friday service. The following may be used as explanations and comments.

INTRODUCTION TO LITURGY

The introduction of the significant parts of the liturgy in the celebrations of Holy Week can be an effective aid to the community. However, they should never try to fully explain or exhaust the meaning of the signs, symbols, or the action being performed.

The season of Lent is quickly drawing to a close and tonight we begin our celebration of the events of our Lord's passion, death, and resurrection. For us, this night has singular importance because it was on this night that our Lord gave us his body and blood in the eucharist as well as the priesthood to continue for future generations the celebration of these sacred realities. Tonight we also recall the service Christ lavished on the apostles by washing their feet; a service meant to dramatize his great love and humility; qualities *we* are now meant to live. The eucharist this evening will be concelebrated in order to manifest more clearly the unity of the priesthood—that all priests share in the one priesthood of Christ.

THEME OF SERVICE

To be read after the homily is finished and after a few moments of silence.

On this night of the commemoration of the Last Supper, priests throughout the world are invited to renew publicly their commitment to priestly ministry as well as to show the dimensions of that service by washing the feet of twelve parishioners. Tonight each of us is called upon to pray for ministers of the word, that the Lord will inspire in them a deep and firm commitment to carry on his ministry of preaching the Gospel, by their words and the example of their lives.

PROCESSION OF THE BLESSED SACRAMENT

(After the celebrant has incensed the Blessed Sacrament, the commentator introduces the procession in his own words. He may use the following as a guideline.)

The body of Jesus which we will receive tomorrow is now carried in procession to the altar of repose. The eucharist is the sign of the salvation we receive from the risen Christ. It tells us again and it tells the world that we are Christ's disciples and that he has made us free to serve him by serving each other.

INTRODUCTION TO MASS

My brothers and sisters, we gather on this holy night to recall the institution of the eucharist by the Lord Jesus on the night before he died. We come to this holy table and throne of God's grace aware of our need for this food and strength from the Lord. May a moment of silence prepare us for the hearing of God's holy word and the reception of this sacred banquet.

PENITENTIAL RITE

You came to do the Father's will: Lord, have mercy . . .

You were the innocent lamb who was slain for our salvation: Christ, have mercy . . .

You transform us by your body and blood into a holy people: Lord, have mercy . . .

GOOD FRIDAY

Historically, the rites surrounding the evolution of this day are ambiguous and varied depending upon the locale and date of the celebration. The elements of the service of the word, the adoration of the cross, the distribution of communion and an afternoon

Vesper service emerge as elements which form the background of the contemporary revision of the liturgy of this day.

The earliest chronicles of this celebration give prominence to two readings, the proclamation of the Passion according to St. John, and the solemn intercessory prayers of the primitive Roman form. These prayers include an invocation and statement of the purpose of the prayer, a pause for silence, and the concluding prayer by the celebrant.

The only day on which this form of the intercessions is prescribed is Good Friday, although this form may be used at other celebrations as well.

The adoration of the cross and the distribution of communion were originally a separate service commemorated in the afternoon about the time when, it was supposed, the crucifixion took place. The evening Vesper service also emerged as a prominent focal point for popular piety. These rites all contribute to the recent revision of the liturgy of Good Friday for the prescription is for the service to be held in the afternoon, and it is composed of an opening prayer, readings, including the Passion according to St. John, the solemn intercessions, the adoration of the cross and the reception of communion.

Theologically this day also has a certain ambiguity and paradox to its theme and orientation. The theme of the day would obviously be one of somber reflections and tragedy if it were to be an historical reminiscence of the death of Jesus. However, the liturgy is not such a reminiscence or re-enactment. While the liturgy is stark in its simplicity and somewhat sober in the reflection it evokes, it is nonetheless a celebration of the paschal mystery—not merely death in isolation. The passion narrative read on Good Friday is from St. John whose clear and constant theology is that the cross is not an instrument of suffering and death, but rather is a sign of hope and victory. The cross is the throne of this King's glory, the place where the manifestation of the glory of the

God-Man takes place for the last time. The crucifixion is not merely the scene of Christ's death; it necessarily points beyond itself to the term of the paschal mystery—the resurrection and glorification of Jesus. It is no longer a place of death; it is the place where death came to an end and life came to all men.

In the revision of the Good Friday liturgy the absence of altar covering is significant as this is the only day in the church year when this is prescribed. Furthermore, the vesture worn by the celebrant is red, a symbol of royalty here, not violet to symbolize penance. The first part of the celebration is the liturgy of the word with its introduction by a silent procession of ministers to the sanctuary, a pause for silence and prostration, and the offering of the opening prayer by the celebrant. A principle of liturgical development is that on the most solemn feasts of the year, the oldest rites and ceremonies are used. This is certainly true of Good Friday for the beginning of the liturgy with the opening prayer and no other ceremonies can be traced as far back as the time of St. Augustine. Also, the use of the Roman form of the intercessions is a more primitive form than the Byzantine litany-type prayers. The literal translation of the opening prayer is useful because of its reference to the paschal mystery, while the alternative form speaks more clearly of the imagery of the sin of Adam, and the likeness of God and man joined in the life of Jesus.

The first reading from the Fourth Servant Song of Isaiah is interpolated again and again in the New Testament to refer to Jesus and is so interpreted by its place and proclamation in the liturgy of Good Friday. He is the perfect servant, who surrendered himself to death that the will of the Father should be accomplished through him.

The reading from the letter to the Hebrews speaks of the priesthood of Christ and that through his obedience to the Father's will he is now able to save all who follow him in obeying the Father. Because of his paschal sacrifice he is now the source of eternal life for all who believe.

The Passion according to St. John is the perfect complement to these readings and the perfect selection for Good Friday since it proclaims Christ as King who resolutely goes to his death for others. There can be no agony in the garden in St. John's Gospel because this is Jesus' finest hour. Jesus is well aware of what is to happen and does not shirk his responsibility but rather is eager to do the will of him who sent him. In the first chapter of this Gospel, John the Baptist bears witness that Jesus is the Lamb of God who takes away men's sins. St. John's Gospel presents the death of the Lamb of God at precisely the time when the passover lambs were slaughtered for Temple sacrifice. The implication of this theology is clear—Jesus is the perfect Lamb of God who obediently goes to the slaughter.

The proclamation of this Gospel in the liturgy indicates clearly that we are not to shun the sacrifice of Jesus at Calvary, but should rather rejoice for they are blessed who find salvation and wash their robes in the blood of the Lamb.

After the proclamation of the Passion (preferably by three readers) the celebrant may preach a brief homily. His comments should underscore the aspect of the cross as the tree of eternal life and the source of salvation; we do not mourn the death of Jesus on Good Friday, instead we acknowledge the cross as our salvation in gratitude and respect.

The general intercessions conclude the liturgy of the word and the celebrant is free to choose from among the ten, those which he understands to be most appropriate for the community.

The veneration of the cross is the second part of the liturgy of Good Friday. The celebrant and ministers take either the veiled or uncovered cross and carry it in procession to the sanctuary, stopping three times to proclaim, "This is the wood of the cross . . ." and inviting the worship of the congregation.

The veneration of the cross can be an effective rite or it can degenerate into mass confusion and boredom. The directives speak of the use of a single cross for the veneration of the congregation. Other crosses may be used if each person is to come forward for the veneration. Another option would be to use the single cross, the one carried in procession, and take it to different parts of the church and ask a group of people at a time to kneel in silence before it. This could be followed at the end of the ceremony with the individual veneration of the cross if the people so wish. This area invites much pastoral adaptation and planning for it to be effective and as complete a sign of reverence for the cross as possible.

The third and final part of the liturgy is the distribution of Holy Communion. The altar is covered for this part of the ceremony with the altar cloth, upon which are placed the corporal and the Sacramentary. The transferral of the Blessed Sacrament from the place of reposition to the altar is accomplished with no ceremony or procession at all. The distribution of the host follows the Our Father, the embolism, and the invitation to partake of the Lamb of God. Both of the prayers after communion are suitable conclusions to the ceremony since they both speak of the resurrection as well as the passion. The prayer is followed by a silent procession of the ministers to the sacristy.

The Easter Triduum lasts until the celebration of the Easter Vigil Mass and the directions of the Sacramentary indicate the kind of activity that is desirable during this time. At the introduction to the celebration of Good Friday, the Sacramentary has the direction that the sacraments are not celebrated on Friday or Saturday and this includes funerals, weddings, and even the sacrament of penance. Pastorally it may be difficult to eliminate the hearing of confessions on these two days, but a positive step in the redirection of pastoral practice regarding penance would be giving the emphasis to a communal celebration of the sacrament of penance of Tuesday or Wednesday of Holy Week, thus imitating the practice of the early church of reconciling penitents before the eucharist on Holy Thursday. Furthermore, the scheduling of weddings should prove no difficulty provided those making the arrangements are aware that weddings are not allowed on these days, for the Sacramentary describes these days of meditation of the events of the passion, death, in anticipation of the resurrection. On Holy Saturday, Holy Communion may only be given as Viaticum.

Guidelines for the celebrant's introduction and comments:

BEFORE THE PROCESSION OF THE MINISTERS

The liturgy of Good Friday is stark in its simplicity and sober in the kind of prayer it evokes. The altar is stripped, and the sanctuary is bare and the central focus of the service is the cross of Christ, the tree of life. Our attention again and again is turned to the sacrifice of the cross where sin and death were conquered and life and love triumphed once and for all. The first part of the liturgy today is a service of the word and begins with a silent procession of the ministers to the altar.

BEFORE THE PROCESSION WITH THE CROSS

The second part of today's service now begins with the procession of the cross. After the priests have venerated the cross you are invited to come forward to venerate or you may venerate it at your place. In the imagery of the book of Genesis it was from a tree that all men sinned; in the imagery of this afternoon's service it is now from the wood of a tree that we are all freed from our sin.

BEFORE HOLY COMMUNION

The third and final part of today's service begins with the preparation of the altar for the distribution of the eucharist. While there is no celebration of the eucharist on Good Friday, we receive communion from the hosts consecrated at the Holy Thursday evening Mass. After the service tonight the eucharist will not be reserved in church and will not be distributed until the Easter Vigil Mass.

CHAPTER V
SEASON OF EASTER

The celebration of the Easter Vigil in the new Sacramentary is placed after the liturgies of Holy Week, and is the beginning of the season of Easter. The Vigil is *the* Christian feast; of new birth, new beginnings, salvation renewed, and humanity restored to the Lord. While it marks the end of the paschal fast, the end of the celebration of Holy Week, and the end of repentance and conversion for which Lent prepared the community, it is much more a beginning. It is the beginning of a new season of grace and a time of joy and thanksgiving, for Easter is not one day or one solemnity—it is a fifty day celebration, and the fifty days from Easter Sunday to Pentecost Sunday together comprise what the General Instruction terms "the great Sunday" (number 22).

From apostolic times the feasts of Easter and Pentecost were primary, and the paschal mystery was the first celebration to have both a time before the feast of preparation and a time afterwards for the extension and completing the celebration. In the new Sacramentary and Lectionary the Sundays following Easter are no longer termed "after" for they are "of" Easter, since they do not follow a solemnity, but they are to be taken as a unity to form one season of solemnity and exaltation at the triumph of Jesus over sin and death.

The new Sacramentary provides a complete Mass formula with opening prayer, prayer over the gifts, and prayer after communion for every day of the fifty days. In the former understanding of the season the feast of the Pentecost was set off because it had its own octave. In the reformed calendar this situation is remedied for the solemnity of the Ascension does not end the season of Easter; it is one special day within an entire special season. The Easter candle is no longer extinguished on the Ascension for it should remain in prominence in the sanctuary until Pentecost and then be placed in the baptistery. It can be used at funerals and at the sacraments of baptism and confirmation. The feast of Pentecost now concludes the Easter season and the week between Ascension and Pentecost should be a time of preparation and expectation for the coming of the Spirit.

The major principle of the calendar reform called for at the Vatican Council—that the paschal mystery be the center of the Christian year—is made obvious in the new Sacramentary because of the emphasis on Easter as the great feast of fifty days.

For the Sundays of Easter, the structure of the Lectionary is changed. The customary first lesson from the Old Testament is eliminated in favor of a reading from the Acts of the Apostles. The gospel reading is taken from the Gospel of St. John, except on the third Sunday of Easter where the appearance of the risen Christ to the apostles on the road to Emmaus is recounted from the Gospel of St. Luke. The reason for this adjustment in what would customarily be readings from the Old Testament and St. Matthew is the fact that from the earliest Lectionary lists available, the reflection of the community was directed toward the beginnings and expansion of the Church in the Acts and readings from St. John, "the spiritual Gospel."

The Easter candle, lighted for the first time from the new fire of the Easter Vigil, is placed in a prominent place in the sanctuary between Easter and Pentecost and should be lighted for all liturgical services in this season and should be incensed whenever incense is used in the fifty days.

The color of the vesture for the season is white, and the cloth or frontal for the altar should be white as well. Liturgical hangings or banners should be made of white and contrasting colors and should reflect the season of new life, fulfillment, rejoicing and joy at the season. Using the same symbols of the Lenten season, e.g., a series of crosses, but changing the colors from penitential violet to the white of Easter, is appropriate. The other tangible sign of the Easter season that should be used to the fullest is water. The use of the rite for blessing and sprinkling with water should be a part of every Sunday eucharist. The introductions to the blessing should be reworded weekly and the prayer for the actual blessing prayer should be taken from that of the Easter season, the third of the options in the Sacramentary.

All penitential elements in the eucharist should be eliminated in this season of sung Alleluias, water, candles and lights. The introductory rite of the eucharist should prepare the community for the sung Glory to God, not merely to have them acknowledge their unworthiness before the experience of God at the eucharist. If at all possible, the congregation should be invited to sing the Glory to God since it falls flat and does not convey its proper significance and exaltation if left to recitation alone, especially in the Easter season.

The season of Easter is *the* season for the sacrament of the eucharist. While recent emphasis on daily reception of the eucharist during Lent has proven to have pastoral benefits, the nature and character of the Easter season almost demands the same emphasis and publicity. Many parishes have inaugurated the practice of preaching at the weekday eucharist only on the weekdays of Advent and Lent. One way to emphasize the Easter season would be to preach daily during this season as well.

The weekday Lectionary contains the continuous reading from the Acts of the Apostles for the first reading and from St. John for the gospel. These sacred books were thought to provide ample instruction and formation during the Easter season for those candidates baptized at the Easter Vigil, and should provide the same formation for those who annually renew their baptismal promises at Easter.

The celebration of a parish First Communion can be introduced and prepared for by a series of para-liturgies on Sunday afternoons during Easter; or even a series of special eucharistic celebrations at a regularly scheduled Sunday liturgy. These can help inform the whole parish of the eucharistic importance of this season as well as link up the preparation of parents and children for the sacrament of the eucharist at the proper liturgical season.

The use of incense at the Sunday liturgies of the Easter season, at least at the main parish eucharist, can help emphasize the importance of this season by sight and smell, as well as by the use of water and light. Current non-use of incense is the apparent custom, and restoring its use on special feasts and seasons can help distinguish certain times from others by a degree of solemnity absent on other feasts.

THE EASTER VIGIL

The night vigil of Easter is *the* feast of Christians. In the words of the *Exsultet:*

> This is our passover feast, when Christ the true lamb is slain, whose blood consecrates the homes of all believers.
>
> This is the night when Christians everywhere, washed clean of sin and freed from all defilement, are restored to grace and grow together in holiness.
>
> It is the night of nights, the highest holy day of the Christian church for we are renewed, made whole again, and reborn in the redemption of Jesus who is raised triumphant from the grave.

According to the new Sacramentary, this is a night vigil and should be so scheduled that the theme of darkness/light becomes obvious; according to the directions, it should not be celebrated before nightfall. It is a night of light, illumination, and rebirth in water and the Spirit. It is a night for initiation, and reinitiation; it is a night of renunciation and allegiance; it is a night of commitment and speaking faith; it is a night of proclamation and exaltation; it is a night of transformation and regeneration.

In the revised rites, the Easter Vigil is composed of four parts, each of which has its own symbolism and richness, yet each of which needs the other part for completion and fulfillment.

THE SERVICE OF LIGHT

This is the first part of the vigil celebration and should begin with the community, or at least a part of the community, gathered outside the church for the blessing of the new fire. The celebrant greets the assembly and introduces them into the celebration of the night watch. The suggested text describes the passing of Jesus from death to life and our identification in passing from sin and evil to new life in Christ at this Vigil.

The celebrant then blesses the fire and lights the Easter candle from the fire. The candle itself is the symbol of Christ; the decorations which customarily decorate the candle are now options. The use of incense and red nails was a conscious attempt to decorate the candle, the symbol of the risen Christ, with the spices and instruments of the passion and burial of Jesus. Depending on local circumstances they may or may not be used. If they are chosen they should be added to the candle before the ceremony so that after blessing of the new fire, the candle is lighted and the procession begins. The deacon, or other minister, takes the candle and begins the procession into the church toward the sanctuary followed by the community who have gathered outside the church for the blessing of the fire. The deacon sings and proclaims "Christ our light" three times, and after the third proclamation the candles of all those in the congregation are lighted from the Easter candle. (The Sacramentary prescribes the use of candles for the congregation.) The deacon then places the candle in the stand, incenses the candle and book, and begins the *Exsultet*, the Easter proclamation. The directions in the Sacramentary indicate that the lights of the church are put on as the candle is placed in the stand. A pastoral adjustment should be made here and the lights left off until after the singing of the Easter proclamation. This gives obvious emphasis to the light of candles, a major symbol of the vigil ceremony. After the singing proclamation, the candles of the congregation are extinguished until the renewal of the baptismal promises.

THE LITURGY OF THE WORD

The second part of the service is the proclamation of the word of God. Nine readings are assigned for this night, seven from the Old Testament and two from the New Testament. The two New Testament readings are prescribed, and some or all of the Old Testament readings may be selected provided the reading about the passage through the Red Sea is among them.

The decision on the number of readings is one that depends on the local circumstance. One way to vary the wordiness that can sometimes be created by reading many of the selections is to vary the response to the readings. After one there can be a sung responsorial psalm, after another a period of silence, after another a recited psalm. Each of the lessons is followed by a collect type of prayer. The reading from the book of Genesis (number 1) about the creation should be read since this is the feast of commemorating origins and redemption. Man was made in the image and likeness of God and renewed in that image through the death and resurrection of God's Son. The obvious imagery of water makes it an appropriate reading for the Easter Vigil. The reading from the book of Exodus 14:15-15:1 is prescribed since it relates the passage of the Israelites through the Red Sea; they walked through water to freedom because of an act of God. The reading of the selection of the prophet Ezekiel is also appropriate since it speaks of the pouring forth of clear water to cleanse the people who had gone astray. The Lord will come and sprinkle clean water on them, give them a clean heart and pour forth his Spirit on them and renew them to live a life according to his statutes. The reading from Romans chapter 6 is the classic text of the Easter Vigil because of the explanation of Christian baptism and the dying and rising asked of a believer as he is plunged into the death and resurrection of Jesus at his baptism. The gospel is taken from St. Matthew and is the account of the resurrection of Jesus and the finding of the empty tomb.

THE LITURGY OF BAPTISM

The third part of the ceremony is the initiation of catechumens into the church by baptism and confirmation and the renewal of the baptismal promises of all the assembly. If at all possible there should be a baptism at the Easter Vigil for this night is, above all else, a baptismal feast. What is especially impressive is the initiation of an adult convert for his initiation can now include water baptism and the administration of the sacrament of confirmation by the celebrant of the liturgy, and the reception of the eucharist for the first time at the Vigil Mass. After the initiation of new members to the community the rest of the community relights their candles from the Easter candle and renews the vows of their baptism.

THE LITURGY OF THE EUCHARIST

The conclusion of the vigil service is the proclamation of the eucharistic prayer and the reception of the paschal communion. The Preface of Easter I is prescribed for the vigil and it speaks of the dying and rising of Jesus. Hence, the second memorial acclamation should be used to respond to the narrative of the Last Supper. The Roman Canon should be used with the proper Communicantes for Easter.

The following may be used as explanatory comments during the Easter Vigil ceremony.

BEFORE THE CEREMONY BEGINS

The first purpose of our Easter Vigil is that like the Jews of old we keep mindful, in faith and gratitude, of all that God has done for us. We commemorate the resurrection of the Lord with all possible solemnity for we cannot forget that through this event we as a people were called to a new life—a life of hope, of joy, and of peace. This is also the night of the great Easter sacraments of baptism and the eucharist—the sacraments that unite us to the bounty of Christ's risen life. As we died with Christ during Lent, we now rise with him to a new life more fully committed to the Father.

The first ceremony of the Easter Vigil is the service of thanksgiving for the light. Here we have the blessing of the new fire which has its roots in the Old Testament, and now, in the Christian usage, is a thanksgiving for Christ who is the true "light of the world."

BEFORE THE READINGS

A brief introduction to the liturgy of the word should be read in accord with the readings selected for proclamation. The following is an example based on the proclamation of five Scripture readings.

In all, there are five readings for our reflection tonight. They span from the creation of the world in the book of Genesis, the passage of the Israelites through the Red Sea, the promise of life in the Spirit in the prophet Ezekiel, to the significance of Christian baptism, and the Easter story as related according to St. Matthew. The theme of all of the readings is the deeds God has worked for us, his people.

BEFORE THE EUCHARIST PRAYER

We now reach the climax of our night watch of the resurrection in the celebration of the eucharistic prayer. The Lamb of God who willed to die upon the cross in the sacrifice of our redemption, who is risen again and lives forever, will now, in the midst of this community and with this community, offer to the Father the eucharistic sacrifice, the great action of thanksgiving. No other eucharist throughout the year is so significant for this is the solemn celebration of Christ's *pasch*—his passage from death to resurrection. Our response to the wondrous mystery in which we are participating is a resounding "Alleluia," Praise to the Lord. May it echo in our hearts and lives through the year.

EASTER SUNDAY

Like the celebration of the Easter Vigil, the celebration of the eucharist on Easter Sunday is a celebration of light and rebirth by water and the Holy Spirit. The Easter candle is placed prominently in the sanctuary and after the renewal of the baptismal promises the celebrant sprinkles the congregation with the water blessed the night before at the Vigil Mass. The directives in the Sacramentary indicate that this renewal of baptismal promises takes the place of the profession of faith and is to be done at all Masses on Easter. Since the use of water is so emphasized at this point in the liturgy, the sprinkling with water should not be used for the introductory rite of the Mass. At the introductory rite the celebrant should acclaim Christ as present as the Risen Lord of this congregation and in this way introduce the sung Glory to God.

The first reading for the liturgy is one of the speeches of the Acts of the Apostles that have been termed "kerygmatic." Like the others in Acts, the speech presents in summary fashion the key to the Christian faith, "Christ has died, Christ is risen, Christ will come again." No other profession or doctrine of the faith comes close to being so central as is the Easter mystery. The reality and substance of the risen body is underscored because Jesus ate and drank after the resurrection. The author is at pains to emphasize who Jesus is, not just what he did on the first Sunday, for he *is* the judge of the living and the dead, he *is* the Lord who grants forgiveness of sins.

The call of Peter in the Acts narrative is a call to us to imitate the apostles in becoming witness of the resurrection, not merely by words but by deeds. This is the theme of both of the Pauline readings assigned to this day, for in both, statements are made about Christ and the believer, and then demands are made upon his witnesses to live their faith. Baptism in the name of Jesus initiates a person into a life lived according to his teaching, and a life of witnessing to his truth. We are to cleanse out the old leaven and replace it with a totally new principle and core of life.

The gospel reading from John shows how Peter himself was transformed from a doubting, hesitant follower, to an active proclaimer, because he saw and believed. He made the decision of faith and did not remain in doubt and uncertainty. Seeing, however, is not believing; Peter decided to become a believer rather than wait for proof. And this decision to believe needed the kind of witnessing in his life that was active and willing. This witnessing began with the speech in Acts. (The Lectionary states that the gospel of the Easter Vigil may be read on Easter morning in place of the Johannine reading; at Masses in the evening the reading of Luke 24:13-35 may replace this gospel. On Easter Sunday in the "A" cycle, this Lukan reading should not be read as it is the focus of the liturgy of the Third Sunday of Easter.)

The opening prayer of the liturgy directs our reflection not only to the event of Jesus' resurrection, but to reflection on what resurrection means, for by it we are all saved and raised to new life in him; his power is now to be at work in us. The alternative wording takes up the ending of the gospel of the day by indicating the necessity of suffering and death to precede the Lord's resurrection, which humiliation must also precede our own exaltation.

The rite for the renewal of baptism vows follows the homily and should be given due emphasis by introducing it as the reason for the Lenten preparation and the reason why Christians gather weekly at the Eucharist.

The first preface of Easter is proclaimed in which the suffering and death of Jesus is mentioned along with his resurrection to new life.

The prayer after communion describes the resurrection as the fulfillment of God's plan of recreating man and restoring him to eternal salvation.

The use of the solemn blessing of Easter Sunday is suggested and should be used because of the solemnity of the occasion.

INTRODUCTION

My friends, we come together this Easter Sunday to celebrate *the* most important day of the Church year—the day when Christ rose for our salvation. In today's liturgy we shall renew the vows of our baptism and recommit ourselves to living the Christian life. As we gather in the name of Christ the Savior let us offer our prayer that by his grace and guidance we will live up to the obligations which this profession of faith entails.

Guidelines for the celebrant's introduction and comments:

PENITENTIAL RITE

All specifically penitential elements of the liturgy should not be emphasized this Sunday. The following is an introduction to the third rite of penance and the Glory to God.

You are the Lamb of God who takes away our sins: Lord, have mercy . . .

You are the risen one who truly makes us live: Christ, have mercy . . .

You rose triumphant on the first Easter day: Lord, have mercy . . .

BEFORE THE READINGS

Today's readings speak as much about the implications of the resurrection of Christ for us who profess faith in Jesus, as they do about the events of the first Easter. Christianity is about acting in faith as much as it is about speaking that faith.

BEFORE THE EUCHARISTIC PRAYER

We gather around this table of the Lord to pray that as these gifts become the body and blood of Christ we might be transformed by this Easter sacrament and live as God's chosen people, as witnesses to his presence among us.

SECOND SUNDAY OF EASTER

With the deliberations and consequent documents of the Second Vatican Council the church of our day has seen major changes in her prayer, organization, and outlook toward the world in which we live. Again and again members of the Church ask for clarification of what has changed and why changes were necessary. Questions such as "Where is it all going?" and "What is it all about?" are asked with greater frequency and intensity. The readings of today's liturgy present a perspective from which we can and should ask such questions.

The first reading from the Acts of the Apostles gives four "marks of the church" which should be obvious hallmarks of her life through all times and places. The major theme is one of fidelity—the act of remaining faithful to an ever-faithful God who invites us to make sure we live according to the profession of faith we made at our baptism. Fidelity is first mentioned in relation to the teaching of the apostles, and St. Luke is at pains in his Gospel and in the Acts to insure his readers that his Gospel is the result of compilation of "eyewitnesses" to the events recorded.

The common life is the second aspect of fidelity and as it was more than an abstract ideal in the early church, it should also be the second characteristic of the present church. Concern for others, love for each other, is the expression of our love of God, and the high esteem in which Christians should be held is due to the example of love and concern they show.

Two other aspects of church life are the breaking of the bread and prayers. Scholars will debate the specific application of these phrases, but what is certain is that table fellowship in the early church was a sign of the Messianic banquet to come in the Kingdom, and the dedication of the first Christians to some form of personal prayer was equally important for them to keep their balance between the concerns of their society and their commitment to the faith.

The second reading of the liturgy from First Peter is written in a context of instruction to those baptized, about the new birth they received and how they should hold to that faith despite trials and harsh sufferings, for sufferings help faith mature.

The gospel reading is the account of the revelation of Jesus in his risen form to Thomas and the confession of Thomas that the Lord is risen. The gospel passage shows that faith does not come because one has seen, but rather because one has heard the word of the Lord and trusts in that revelation. The example of Thomas is that he who had faith in Jesus before the resurrection had to remake that confession for it to be a mature and personal belief. We ourselves need to make our acts of faith repeatedly because faith is a process, not a state; it is a process where the profession of faith is not easily made, especially when we are faced with suffering and difficulty.

The opening prayer of the liturgy makes reference to the baptismal setting of First Peter where sin is washed away and we receive new birth in the Spirit. The alternate wording speaks more specifically of the risen life we share in Christ and tells us that we should look for his presence among the living, not the dead.

The prayer over the gifts speaks of both baptism as initiation and the eucharist as a continual sacrament of belief and faith profession.

The prayer after communion describes these as the Easter sacraments, the means by which we communicate with the risen Christ. The preface of the day is the first of the Easter season and the solemn blessing is that for the Easter season.

Guidelines for the celebrant's introduction and comments:

INTRODUCTION

My friends, we come together at the eucharist to speak our faith, and to renew and deepen our trust in God. We come with our doubts and misgivings and know that our faith is not as strong as it should be. But still we come to experience the presence of God with us, and that because of his presence we may be made strong and firm in our conviction that he is our Savior. As we pray that this water be blessed, we pray as well that we may be made more aware of the presence of God among us.

BEFORE THE READINGS

Our generation of Catholics has seen many changes and adjustments in the "faith of our fathers." In the liturgy of the world today we are presented with certain hallmarks of the Church whatever the time and place in history. These readings serve to help us understand the things that really matter and those things which can quite legitimately pass away.

SIGN OF PEACE

May we who receive his peace and love in this sacrament offer to each other a sign that will work to spread his peace in our world.

THIRD SUNDAY OF EASTER

Since the approval and promulgation of the Constitution on the Sacred Liturgy, there has been a major shift in liturgical piety. The new orientation is away from emphasizing the validity of a sacrament and rubrical perfection in the "performance" of a sacrament, to one that is concerned with an experience of the risen Lord and the quality of the celebration as an act of thanksgiving and praise of the community to the Father. The gospel story related on this third Sunday of Easter presents a moving portrayal of the experience of the risen Lord with two of his disciples on the road to Emmaus. This pericope is so important for the development of the Easter season that it is now read at a Sunday eucharist whereas formerly it was used on the Monday after Easter Sunday. While a basic theme of the readings of Easter is water and baptism, this gospel presents us with another theme where the eucharist is the sacrament which continues and deepens what was pledged at the font of baptism. The very style of the gospel story shows that it is a special resurrection appearance story, for the references to their hearts burning when he explained the word and their recognizing him at the breaking of the bread indicate that the author refers here to the experience of Christ as the eucharist.

The proclamation of the word was much more than something that would lead to intellectual assent; rather it caused the hearts of the apostles to burn with hope and enthusiasm. Then the revelation of the risen Christ was made clear in the breaking of the bread; the man teacher became their risen Lord at the moment of the eucharistic banquet.

Such is our own experience, for we read the Scriptures for our formation and guidance, and we present bread and wine that they become the very presence of Christ.

The other two readings for this Sunday continue the lectionary principles for the season. The first reading is the speech of Peter about key points in the profession of faith in the life, suffering and resurrection of Jesus. The second reading is a continuation of the first letter of Peter where the believer who has been given deliverance and the gift of salvation at baptism is required to live according to that experience of God with him. The use of the image of the blood of the Lamb provides an important link between baptism and the eucharist. Just as the convert receives new life at baptism because of the sacrifice of Jesus, the readings speak as well of the coming of the full reign where the believer continually shares in that redemption by sharing in the blood of the Lamb of God at the eucharist.

The prayers of the liturgy in the Sacramentary have clear eucharistic associations; but they speak not merely of remembering the past sacrifice of Jesus, they speak as well of the coming of the full reign of God at the end of time. The alternative wording of the opening prayer is preferable because it speaks of the word of God and expresses the request that we who witness to the resurrection of Jesus may rise from the realm of death with him in a like resurrection.

The prayer over the gifts notes the eschatological reference of the eucharist by speaking of the perfect joy to be shared in heaven.

Any of the Easter prefaces may be used but the third is most appropriate because it speaks of the Lamb of God, Christ as victim, priest and advocate interceding on our behalf.

The blessing provided in the Sacramentary is one of the prayers over the people and should be replaced by the solemn blessing of the Easter season since the structure of the solemn blessing should be used throughout the Easter season until Pentecost Sunday.

Guidelines for the celebrant's introduction and comments:

INTRODUCTION

The resurrection of Christ from the dead is not the end of the story of his saving work for us, his people. We come to worship him each week in the knowledge that he continues to redeem us by making intercession on our behalf before the Father in heaven. May we who are blessed with this water be made conscious of the presence of God in our midst this day in his word and this sacrament of his body and blood.

BEFORE THE READINGS

Personal experiences often leave the fondest of memories because we met a friend, truly communicated with a person, or came to realize the true worth of a person. In today's readings we are reminded that we meet the Lord and experience his presence in the readings at the eucharist as well as in his body and blood. We should not take his words lightly because they are for our formation as well as our consolation.

BEFORE THE EUCHARISTIC PRAYER

The Lamb who was slain for our salvation and who came to take our sins away is the Lamb whose body and blood we share at the eucharist. May we come to recognize the powerful presence of God in our midst in this bread of life and cup of everlasting salvation.

FOURTH SUNDAY OF EASTER

"Good Shepherd Sunday" was formerly celebrated on the second Sunday after Easter (the Sunday following Low Sunday). In the revised Lectionary and Sacramentary this image of Jesus is the basis of reflection on this fourth Sunday of Easter instead. In all three Sunday cycles of readings, parts of the Johannine discourse are read: year "A" John 10:1-10, year "B" John 10:11-18, year "C" John 10:27-30. Some of the biblical images of the Lord, especially those of the sower and the shepherd, are often difficult to translate to a society as modernized, sophisticated, and institutionalized as ours. And yet, the curious thing about the image of the Good Shepherd is that despite some problems in translation it is among the most appealing of New Testament images for it presents Christ as actively searching out the lost, not to bring them to trial and cross-examination, but to return them to the fold. Christ is indeed the only shepherd who is rightfully called "Good" because he leaves behind the "saved" of the flock and looks after the lost. By any other accounting the shepherd should be glad only one of the flock was lost and be satisfied with ninety-nine in his possession. Despite the fact that sound economics would recommend it, this state of affairs is not tolerated by the good shepherd.

The reading of the end of Peter's speech, begun in last week's first reading, has little connection with the rest of the readings about the shepherd. The responsorial psalm introduces the shepherd theme with Psalm 23, and the second reading from First

Peter ends with a reference to the shepherd as the guardian of the community. The first ten verses of the "good shepherd" chapter of John's Gospel speak about Christ as the gate of the sheepfold, and as the keeper of the sheep. Salvation is offered only for those who call upon his name, for he is the only perfect sacrifice acceptable to the Father. As members of his flock, we gain salvation through him.

The prayers in the Sacramentary are replete with references to the readings of this Sunday since all three years contain the same theme in the readings.

The opening prayer invokes Christ as the shepherd who leads us to the Father, and the phrasing is that of the Gospel of John. The alternative wording of the prayer uses the language of the responsorial psalm. The selection of which prayer to use depends on the theme of the celebrant's homily.

The preface may be chosen from any of the Easter prefaces, but the second, with a reference to the "gates of heaven," or the third with reference to Christ as the Lamb, priest, advocate and victim, seem most appropriate.

The prayer after communion speaks of the eternal shepherd who feeds the flock of Christ with the eucharist as a foretaste of the bounty of the promised land in the kingdom.

The solemn blessing of the Easter season is printed in the text of this Sunday and should be used.

Guidelines for the celebrant's introduction and comments:

INTRODUCTION

My brothers and sisters, we come together each week at the eucharist to have our vision cleared and our perspective adjusted according to the word of God, as well as to partake in the banquet of his body and blood. We come to worship the Father today through Jesus, the Savior, the Good Shepherd. As we prepare to hear the word of God this day, let us pause and ask the Father to help us realize in our lives his way, his truth, and his life.

BEFORE THE READINGS

A person's image of God needs constant evaluation and refinement according to the word of God so that he not get lost in speculation and blind alleys. In today's readings Christ the Good Shepherd reveals himself as a shepherd who never leaves his flock without his guidance, love, and support.

BEFORE THE EUCHARISTIC PRAYER

Just as the Good Shepherd seeks out the lost members of his flock, the Lord Jesus seeks to heal us and bind up our wounds by the sacrament of his body and blood. It is fitting that we should gather now to offer him our prayer of praise, glory, homage, and thanksgiving.

FIFTH SUNDAY OF EASTER

In the reform of the sacraments called for at the Second Vatican Council, one major emphasis has been that sacraments are community celebrations, not just private enterprises between the minister and the person on whom a sacrament is conferred. The very structure of the initiation of adults into the Church envisions the active involvement of people at the scrutinies on the Sundays of Lent and their support at the ceremony of baptism. The celebration of the eucharist has been so revised that lectors, cantors, servers, ushers, artists, and musicians all have a proper and significant role to play in what was once regarded as the priest's preserve. The faith of the community and their participation as a priesthood of the faithful is most important for post-Vatican II sacramental theology. One of the texts most often used to present this notion of the faithful's priesthood is the end of today's second reading.

The reading from the Acts of the Apostles is a difficult text for New Testament scholars for the exact "institution" of the diaconate and the real exercise of that ministry in the early Church is disputed. Whether or not seven men were set aside for the temporal affairs is hard to substantiate. What is one clear intent in the passage, however, is the establishment that charitable concerns are not foreign to the sacred community of believers and that there must be an obvious connection between the affairs of God and the affairs of men. This service theme is carried through in First Peter where the result of a person's baptism joins him to a community and the concerns of another become as real as one's own.

The part of the text, "chosen race, royal priesthood, holy nation, God's own people" needs careful examination because it is often cited and even over-used. The connotation is that a chosen race is also a race of mutual service; a royal priesthood is also a community of humble servants; and God's own people set apart for the things of the Lord are at the same time a people who must live and work among people of all persuasions. It is precisely amid that diversity that the believer must show forth his Christianity. But the real key to all of these titles for the people of God is that they all hinge on holiness. Being initiated into the community, the priesthood of the faithful, means that there must always be a constant and continual growth in holiness. God has acted out of his boundless love in making us part of his family, so we are to grow in holiness to share that love with others. This growth in holiness is not a clerical or "religious" preserve for the context for this exhortation from First Peter is the setting of communal instruction of all the baptized.

The gospel gives the areas that one should check in his progress in sanctity. To what extent is a pious exercise or act of charity helping one grow in the way, truth, and life of the Lord? In one sense, we are all deacons, dedicated to works of charity, and yet we are all contemplatives, dedicated to growth in holiness and personal prayer.

Both texts of the opening prayer of the liturgy present a general theme for prayer rather than a specific reference to the readings of the day. The prayer over the gifts speaks of the exchange of gifts, bread and wine, becoming the body and blood of Christ. The prayer also uses the Johannine terminology of the gospel to speak of the Lord's truth.

The recommendation in the Sacramentary is that one of the Easter prefaces should be used this Sunday. However, because of the verbal identification of the second reading with the first preface for Sundays in ordinary time, this preface should be used.

The prayer after communion continues this relationship of the prayer over the gifts to the gospel by speaking of new life in Christ because of the reception of the eucharist.

The suggested blessing of the day is taken from the prayers over the people and should be replaced by the solemn blessing of the Easter season.

Guidelines for the celebrant's introduction and comments:

INTRODUCTION

Especially on this Sunday when the theme of the liturgy is found explicitly in the second reading about the obligations of one's baptism, the use of the rite of blessing and sprinkling with holy water is in order.

My friends, in today's second reading we who are baptized in Christ are called "a chosen race" for the service of each other, "a royal priesthood," yet should reject no menial task; "God's own people," but we should not hide behind this title as if it were a protection. We pray that as we ask the Father to bless and consecrate this water for our use, he might bless and consecrate us who are signed with this water to be servants of his will in our world.

BEFORE THE READINGS

In a society such as ours which highly regards rank and prestige as terms of honor, the demands of Jesus to surrender all for his service is a penetrating and difficult task. We who were reborn in baptism are asked in today's readings to remake our whole lives after the pattern of Jesus' willing service and love for the least of the brothers.

BEFORE THE EUCHARISTIC PRAYER

Growth in holiness demands that we imitate the Lord of us all in prayer and work. As we offer this great eucharistic prayer may we be transformed by the body and blood of Christ into willing servants of his will.

SIXTH SUNDAY OF EASTER

In the norms for the liturgical year in the General Instruction (number 26), the time between the solemnity of the Ascension and the vigil of Pentecost is a time of preparation and expectation for the coming of the Holy Spirit. This emphasis on the coming of the Paraclete begins a week earlier in the Lectionary since today's readings all speak of the coming of "another Paraclete," the "Spirit of truth" and the living Spirit of God.

In the first reading from the Acts of the Apostles, Peter and John are sent from Jerusalem to Samaria to be ministers of the coming of the Spirit to the new converts in that town. These men had already been baptized in the name of the Lord Jesus, and the imposition of hands completes the initiation of these converts. It would be an anachronism, however, to speak of the coming of the Spirit at the laying on of hands as our present sacrament of confirmation.

For St. Luke there is no such distinction, and his concern is to emphasize the work of the Spirit in convert-making and in personal conversion rather than to distinguish moments and times of what has come to be two sacraments of initiation in the later Church. According to Luke, the Spirit is the source of vitality for the believing Church after the resurrection of Jesus and the work of the Spirit is the cause for the missionary expansion of Christianity; for Luke, the time of the Church is the age of the Spirit (H. Conzelmann).

The reading from First Peter indicates that baptism initiates a person to imitation of the death and resurrection of Jesus and that the destiny of all believers is to live according to the realm of the Spirit.

In the gospel of John the coming of the Paraclete means the coming of the promised Counselor and Advocate whose power enlivens the community of believers. Jesus must leave the Church so that a new appearance and manifestation of the power of God can take place. The link for all three readings is that the Paraclete is soon to come to strengthen us in our profession of the faith.

The prayers from the Sacramentary do not reflect the theme of the readings but are of a general nature and theme.

The eucharist is an Easter sacrament according to the prayer after communion and it is an agent of sin forgiveness in the prayer over the gifts.

The alternate form of the opening prayer uses death and resurrection as one theme, and this pattern is repeated in the second preface for the Easter season which can be chosen for proclamation.

The solemn blessing of the Easter season is suggested in the Sacramentary and should be used throughout the Easter season.

Guidelines for the celebrant's introduction and comments:

INTRODUCTION

The following is a suggested introduction to the blessing and sprinkling with Holy Water.

The Christian faith is a profession of faith in the name of God the Father, through the Son, in the power of the Holy Spirit. In today's gospel, St. John calls the Holy Spirit the Paraclete, the Advocate, and the Counselor who is forever with the community of believers to assist them in their profession and lives of faith. As we ask the Spirit to bless this water which we will use to renew our baptismal faith, may we also realize the power of the Holy Spirit at work in our midst this day to lead us to the Father through his risen Son, Jesus Christ.

BEFORE THE READINGS

The making of a Christian is a task that takes a life-time. In today's readings it is the power of the Spirit of truth who helps men in their continual process of turning from the ways of the world to the way of Christ and his Gospel. The true believer is not one who merely speaks his faith; he is one who obeys the commandments of the Lord, guided by the Paraclete, the Spirit of truth.

BEFORE THE EUCHARISTIC PRAYER

In this prayer of praise and thanksgiving we pray that the Spirit may make these gifts of bread and wine the sacrifice acceptable to the Father. We pray as well that we who receive this eucharist may offer ourselves as living sacrifices to the Father in the quality and manner of our lives when this Mass has ended.

SOLEMNITY OF THE ASCENSION

The celebration of this feast can easily degenerate into an historical reminiscence of the event of Jesus taking leave of his first followers. The true nature and theme of the feast, however, is anything but this kind of recollection. The Ascension is not merely a day of departure; it is rather a day of commissioning and sending the apostles forth to continue to preach the reign of God. In all three cycles of the Lectionary the first two readings are the same from Acts and Ephesians, but the Gospel reading changes with each year.

This year's gospel is the conclusion of St. Matthew's Gospel and contains many important Matthean stylistic traits. The setting of the sending forth is a mountain, an important place of revelation throughout the Scriptures, from the giving of the Torah to Moses on Mt. Sinai, to the preaching of the beatitudes by Jesus at the sermon on the mount, to the missionary discourse in this reading. The apostles fall down in homage as a profession of faith in the risen Lord, but Matthew adds the note that some of these men also "doubted." This is not the first time that the evangelist does this for in the miracle of the stilling of the storm in Matthew 8:23-27 the apostles, the ones who should have had a firm faith and confidence in Jesus, are precisely the ones who are remonstrated because of their "little faith." The lesson involved here is that the presence of doubts and fears will beset believers in every age and they should not let that paralyze them, for this was the experience of the earliest apostles as well. Faith in any age has its insecurities and problems.

The commission and sending forth of the apostles is the main point of the story as they are sent to make other disciples by their preaching and example. The spread of Christianity from a ghettoized Judaism is the theme of the Acts of the Apostles as enunciated in the first reading of today's liturgy, and it is the charge given to the apostles by Jesus. The command is to teach all that Jesus taught, and to baptize men in his name. The support and strength they will need for this task in the early Church is the same for all ages because the Gospel specifically refers to the presence of Emmanuel, "I am with you always," which itself is a reference to the early chapters of Matthew which declare that the Messiah will reign with us forever.

The prayers of the liturgy in the Sacramentary indicate that our ascension to the Father is our destiny, just as Jesus' ascension and return to the Father was his destiny. In the prayer after communion the divine life we share in the eucharist is a foretaste of the eternal life we will share in the kingdom.

The preface may be either of those assigned to the time of Ascension but the better choice is the first where the ascension is not interpreted as an abandonment of the Church but rather as the going forth of Jesus to prepare a place for all those who one day will join him in the kingdom.

While formerly the Easter candle was to be extinguished after the proclamation of the gospel on the solemnity of the Ascension, the directives now state that the Easter season continues to the solemnity of Pentecost. Hence, the prescribed sanctuary decor until Pentecost includes the paschal candle and should include all other hangings and appointments which have been used since Easter.

Guidelines for the celebrant's introduction and comments:

INTRODUCTION

To show that this feast is now part of a continuity of the whole Easter season, the rite of water blessing should be used on this day as well as on the Sundays of the Easter season.

At the completion of every celebration of the eucharist we are charged to go forth and live the sacred mysteries we have just celebrated. This commission was first given to the disciples when Jesus ascended to his Father.

As we commemorate the solemnity of the Ascension at this eucharist today, let us realize that we are sent forth to be the presence of the Lord in a world that needs his healing, his love, and his understanding. We now pray that God will bless this water and in turn bless each of us so we may fulfill the command of the Gospel to be his witnesses strengthened by the presence of his body and blood at this eucharist.

BEFORE THE READINGS

(While the main theme of the readings and the nature of the solemnity points to emphasis on the missionary command of Jesus and the commissioning of all believers, a second theme from the reading from Ephesians about the Church as the Body of Christ can be utilized. The introduction to the reading should be composed in light of the theme of the homily of the day.)

BEFORE THE FINAL BLESSING

Just as the disciples were sent forth in today's gospel to teach all that Jesus had taught them, the blessing we receive this day will make us servants of his word. Our preaching is by the kind of life that we lead. Our preaching is by example, far more than by our words.

SEVENTH SUNDAY OF EASTER

Since the octave of Pentecost and the concept of Sundays after Pentecost have been eliminated in the new calendar, this Sunday should appropriately emphasize the coming of the Spirit, and the watchfulness and prayer which marked the days prior to the first Pentecost.

The first reading from the Acts of the Apostles describes our own situation as well as the situation of the early community. These men first gathered in the upper room for the Last Supper with Jesus and now gather together again to await the gift of his Holy Spirit. The same is true of the present Church for we gather at the eucharist to proclaim the death of the Lord and we celebrate this Sunday in particular to await the coming of the Paraclete. In the plan of the author of St. Luke's Gospel and the Acts the city of Jerusalem, the site of the upper room, is as much a theologically significant place as it is important as a center of the culture of the day. In the Gospel, Jesus is portrayed as making his way to this city to suffer and die; and in the Acts it is from this city that the apostles are sent forth to bring the Gospel to the ends of the earth. In the reading from Acts, a chief characteristic of the apostles is their prayer, a theme which is returned to again and again in the book of Acts to indicate important events in the life of the Church. Most particularly, the community spends time in prayer before laying hands on ministers of the word or sending them forth to preach.

The reading from First Peter returns to a frequently enunciated theme in the letter, that suffering for the faith is to be part of the life of a believer. Just as Holy Week cannot be fully understood without constant attention to the event of Easter, so the glory and joy of the Easter season cannot be appreciated fully without bringing attention to the fact that the follower of Jesus must walk in trial and suffering as well. The theme of the unity of suffering and glorification is a major theme of the Gospel of John from which today's gospel reading is taken. This part of the gospel has been aptly described as the "last will and testament" of Jesus (E. Käsemann). The "hour" of Jesus had finally come—the hour of triumph, glory, and the exaltation of Jesus. And yet, for St. John this hour of glory is the hour of Jesus' death as well. At Cana Jesus protested that his hour had not yet come; now it is upon him, that through the cross he may call all men to his Father. The gospel also parallels the reading from the Acts since the setting of the proclamation of Jesus is his prayer for his followers. He prays for those whom the Father has given him, that while still in the world, they may not become part of the world. The trial for the believer is to remain faithful to the word of God while still living in the imperfect world of the non-believer. (The unifying theme of all the readings is a prayerful expectation for the coming of the Spirit who will keep believers faithful to the word of God, despite suffering and trial.)

The prayers of the Sacramentary coincide more accurately with the theme of glory from the gospel for in the opening prayer the eucharist is the setting of a present sharing in the glory of Christ; in the prayer over the gifts the eucharist is a foretaste of the eternal glory of the kingdom; and in the prayer after communion, the glory of the risen Christ is given to the Church to share at the sacrament of the Lord's body and blood.

The second preface for the Ascension could be used since it locates the celebration between the ascension of Christ and the coming of the Spirit, and the solemn blessing for Ascension could also be used in place of the suggested prayer over the people. (If this solemn blessing is used, the words of the first invocation might be adjusted to this time of the Ascension rather than the day of his ascension.)

Guidelines for the celebrant's introduction and comments:

INTRODUCTION

My friends, we gather as did the first followers of Jesus between his ascension and the event of Pentecost to pray and watch for the manifestation of the power of the Holy Spirit. May we who come to share in the glory of the risen Christ at this holy banquet also be willing to endure the trials and suffering which are part of the Christian life.

BEFORE THE READINGS

The themes for the exploration of the preacher on this Sunday include the necessity of suffering and enduring trial to be a true Christian, the attitude of the believer who waits in prayer for the coming of the Spirit, and that the hour of Jesus to show his glory is also the hour of his death on the cross. Depending on the theme of the homily, this introduction can serve to point the attention of the congregation to one of these themes.

BEFORE THE EUCHARIST PRAYER

The Christian lives between two times—between the incarnation of the Lord and his final coming in glory. As we offer our prayer of praise and thanksgiving to the Father for this sacrament of salvation, let us pray as well that the Spirit who is to come to us at Pentecost may confirm and strengthen our lives of faith.

SOLEMNITY OF PENTECOST

There is a tendency in the interpretation of the Christian liturgy to historicize feasts and seasons in order to dramatize or recreate again events as they once happened in sacred history. And yet, the liturgy itself resists quite strongly any theology which would support this kind of activity. The season of Advent is a time of preparation for Christ as he comes to us now, and as he will come to us, not as he came two thousand years ago. The celebrations of

Holy Week are understood together, for the paschal mystery is a unit, no one event is isolated from the others. The celebration of Pentecost is not the historical reminiscence of the first Pentecost either. The festival of Pentecost is a completion, for the Spirit is given anew to those who believe in order that they might complete God's work on earth. The Spirit is a gift, but not a possession to be selfishly hoarded. The Spirit is manifested only in our giving.

The first reading for this Sunday recounts the event of the first Pentecost, a feast which had its Jewish roots and came to be celebrated as a renewal of the Covenant between God and the People of Israel, and a specific recollection of the giving of the Law to Moses at Sinai. The Christian observance is marked by the recounting in this reading of the descent of the Spirit but in style and content the reading recalls the Old Testament account of the Tower of Babel where men became confused by their own stubborn wills; but with the coming of the Spirit, this confusion is ended and barriers of language and nationality are no more.

The responsorial psalm summarizes the nature of the day as it prays that the Spirit come now to renew the face of the earth. Just as the Spirit hovered over the waters at the dawn of creation, as Jesus gave up his spirit at his death on the cross, and as the apostles received the Spirit at Pentecost, we pray this psalm that the world may be enlivened by that same recreative Spirit. This power of God was active before time was, was active as well in historical time in the life of Jesus, and will be active for all time among those who believe.

The reading from First Corinthians speaks of the Spirit as the bond of unity, despite the different gifts and talents of the community. The differences between Jew and Greek, male and female will remain, but the Spirit will bind all together in something which is far more important than uniformity of action and will. There will and should be differences, but the Spirit is over all, not to stifle anyone but to bring all gifts together for the good of all.

The gospel proclamation ties in with the story of the creation of man in the book of Genesis, for as Yahweh breathed into the clay of the earth and made man, so Jesus the God-Man breathed on the apostles to commission them to go forth to proclaim his peace.

In the opening prayer of the Sacramentary, the Spirit is envisioned as preaching through the believing Church to show the present reality of the power of God. The alternative wording, however, is much more appropriate for it is filled with biblical and liturgical imagery. It proclaims God as the Father of *light*, a reference to the termination of the Easter season; to the *wind* and *flame* of the first Pentecost of the first reading; to the *peace* which he brings as seen in the gospel reading; to the *love* which binds all together in the reading from St. Paul. It may be that the prayer has too many allusions and therefore is difficult to understand, but if proclaimed slowly and distinctly, can be a very effective opening to the celebration.

The preface of Pentecost is prescribed for use and shows this day as the completion of the Easter season for now it is the Spirit who continues to renew the face of the world.

The prayer after communion speaks of the vigor of the Spirit to initiate our mission, and the gifts we possess which are varied but which are to be used in the work of evangelization.

The solemn blessing of Pentecost is prescribed for use and is filled with biblical imagery about the Spirit. It should also be proclaimed slowly and distinctly.

The following may be used as explanations and comments.

INTRODUCTION

Today we celebrate the feast of the coming of the Holy Spirit upon the apostles and upon the Church. We come to reflect on the vocation that the Spirit has given to us at baptism and confirmation, to continue his work in this world. As the Lord renews us by this sacrament of his body and blood, let us pray that through us he will renew the face of the world.

BEFORE THE READINGS

To a world as broken and divided as ours, to speak of unity and common purpose seems almost hopeless. It is only by the power of the Holy Spirit that we, who are the pilgrim Church, may ever hope to realize the kind of unity the Scriptures speak of. We are invited in these readings to realize that the unity of the Spirit does not do away with differences; it rather brings them all together to make our varied talents serve the proclamation of his Gospel.

BEFORE THE EUCHARISTIC PRAYER

In this prayer of praise and thanksgiving, we ask that the Spirit come upon these gifts to make them the sacrament of our salvation, and that he will come upon us as well to make us living witnesses of his presence in this world.

BEFORE THE SIGN OF PEACE

May our sign of peace this day be a sign of our respect for each other and our common commitment to spread the kingdom of God with the help of each other. Let us offer each other the sign of peace.

CHAPTER VI
SUNDAYS IN ORDINARY TIME

The cycle of Sundays "throughout the year" or in ordinary time is one of the changes in the reformed liturgy. The Sundays between Epiphany and Lent had been noted as Sundays after Epiphany, and the Sundays between Pentecost and the season of Advent were called Sundays after Pentecost. With the revision of the calendar, the clear emphasis on these Sundays is not on the seasons or feasts which they follow, but on the Scripture readings proclaimed on the day. The Lectionary receives precedence and priority, and the prayers and options from the Sacramentary are to be selected to correspond, where possible, to these readings.

The principle of the Lectionary which determines the Sunday readings "in ordinary time" is different from that which governs the readings of a liturgical season. For special seasons and feasts, a single theme runs through the readings. For the Sundays in ordinary time the readings present two themes for consideration. The first and major theme is that of the gospel, the Old Testament lesson, and the responsorial psalm. For the Sundays of the "A" cycle the gospel is from St. Matthew in semi-continuous selections. The Old Testament lesson and psalm are chosen to correspond with the gospel of the day. The second reading presents the alternative theme, and for the "A" cycle it is taken from Epistles attributed to St. Paul. From the second to the eighth Sundays, the reading is from First Corinthians, from the ninth to the twenty-fourth Sundays it is from the Epistle to the Romans, from the twenty-fifth to the twenty-eighth Sundays it is from the Letter to the Philippians, and for the remaining Sundays, leading up to the feast of Christ the King, this reading is from First Thessalonians. On these Sundays all three readings should not be made to harmonize since this second lesson is clearly devoted to another theme. It is for this reason that the commentary which follows for these Sundays emphasize the gospel theme and notes the alternate theme of the second reading separately.

The revised Sacramentary provides a number of new elements in the liturgy which may be used to coincide with the Scripture readings of the Sunday. In the revised Order of Mass, there are appended to "penitential rites" eight sets of invocations before the "Lord, have mercy." The Sunday preface may now be chosen from eight possibilities, each of which refers to a different aspect of salvation through the paschal mystery of Jesus. The blessings at the end of Mass may take the form of prayers over the people or solemn, three-part blessings. It would be appropriate to keep the structure of the solemn blessing for special seasons and solemnities and the prayers over the people for these Sundays of the year. In all, there are twenty-four such prayers for blessings.

The most important thing for the parish committee to determine for the planning of the Sunday eucharist is what readings the celebrant will emphasize in the preaching of the day. The selection of music, explanatory comments, introductions, and the prayer of the faithful all depend on this basic choice. One suggestion for these Sundays might be to determine whether the parish should concentrate on the second reading for several Sundays and then return to the gospel as the basis for the celebration of the other Sundays of the year. For example, a parish may want to emphasize the reading from First Corinthians for the second through the eighth week and then devote attention to the gospel readings from Matthew for the rest of the year. One of the purposes of the Lectionary revision is to provide common reflection on a given scriptural book at a time.

SECOND SUNDAY IN ORDINARY TIME

It may seem a bit curious to begin the "season of the year" with the second Sunday, rather than the first. In reality, however, the first Sunday of the year is the feast of the Baptism of the Lord and this second Sunday continues that theme with a consideration of the incarnation of the servant, Jesus.

The reading of the Second Servant Song of Isaiah clearly reflects the theme of the Epiphany about salvation to the ends of the earth. The servant of Yahweh is the one who is a light to all the nations so that the saving power of God may reach to the ends of the earth. The gospel reading of the day is the single exception to the rule that all the readings of the "A" cycle for the Sundays of the year come from St. Matthew's Gospel. There is no explicit recounting in St. John's Gospel of the baptism of Jesus, but this reading comes closest to it. The servant of the first reading is described here as the Lamb of God who takes away men's sins. The incarnation of the Savior is to be understood now in terms of the redemption he was sent to accomplish; the birth of the Messiah leads to the death and resurrection of this servant that all men might be saved through that one sacrifice.

The responsorial psalm links the two readings since the refrain is "Here am I, Lord, I come to do *your* will."

The lesson of the readings is that Jesus was the perfect servant of the Father, and that we too come to be servants of the Father's will, strengthened by the blood of the Lamb of God. Jesus was the only servant of the Father ever to fulfill completely the prayer "Your will be done," for he freely accepted and gave himself up to death that others might share life through that sacrifice.

The second theme of the liturgy is taken from the beginning of First Corinthians, portions of which letter will be read for the next six Sundays. The community at Corinth may best be described as a feeble church of sinners. Nonetheless, Paul addressed them as "holy" because they call on the name of the Lord Jesus Christ. The introductory greeting of this Epistle has been adapted as one of the greetings for the beginning of the eucharist and should be used this Sunday, "the grace and peace of God our Father and the Lord Jesus Christ be with you." Sending greetings of grace and peace are standard introductions to the Epistles and some consideration of what these mean might prove helpful to the congregation. The Corinthian church is called a part of the Church of God, but only a part of the whole. There is no such thing in Paul's terminology as a church in isolation either from other churches or the rest of the world.

The opening prayers of the liturgy are both introduced by references to the peace of Christ. The first form speaks of the grace and peace of the second reading, but the alternate wording is preferable if the theme of the liturgy is taken from the gospel reading. In it we pray that the Father will help us submit to his will as did the servant Jesus, the Lamb of God.

The preface for this Sunday is to be taken from those for the Sundays of the year and number III, about salvation from a man like us, the Lamb of God, or number VII, about restoration through the obedience of Christ, are those which coincide best with the readings.

The prayer over the people, number 11, could be used as a fitting conclusion to a celebration focused on our obedience to the Father's will.

The dismissal for the eucharist could be the third option, that the community may go in peace (the first reading) to love and serve the Lord (the first and gospel readings).

Guidelines for the celebrant's introduction and comments:

INTRODUCTION

My brothers and sisters, we gather around the table of the Lord to celebrate this memorial sacrifice of the redemption of Jesus Christ offered to us now through the body and blood of the Lamb of God. May our participation in the life and death of the servant Jesus help us in offering ourselves as servants of the will of God our Father.

PENITENTIAL RITE

You came to teach us the Father's will: Lord, have mercy . . .

You willingly gave your life for our salvation: Christ, have mercy . . .

You are the Lamb of God who takes away our sins: Lord, have mercy . . .

BEFORE THE READINGS

Every time we gather for the celebration of the eucharist we pray that the Lamb of God may take away our sins and have mercy on us. The Scripture readings today show us that we are sharers in the redemption accomplished in Christ because he was the perfect servant of the will of our Father.

BEFORE THE LORD'S PRAYER

Before we share in communion of the one bread and cup of our salvation, let us call upon the Father and pray that his will may be accomplished through us on earth, as it was in the life of his Son and our Lord.

THIRD SUNDAY IN ORDINARY TIME

Conventional descriptions of the ministry of priests, as of any preachers of the word of God, have often been couched in terms of distinctions between the body/soul, flesh/spirit, natural/supernatural. The minister who concerned himself with the liberation of the oppressed, the freedom of the underprivileged, or the equality of the races, was often thought to be doing good work, but not the specific work of the minister of God.

The gospel lesson of this Sunday breaks down such precise distinctions by presenting Jesus as more than a rabbi, teacher, or preacher of a new way of life. Christianity is no detached philosophical system or set of propositions. Its concern is with whole people, and making them whole, not just improving their mental capacities and thought processes. Jesus is the preacher of the new kingdom, the herald of Good News of the Father, but he is equally the healer who binds up the wounds of those in need.

The alleluia verse of the liturgy sums up the gospel proclamation by stating that Jesus preached the Gospel and healed the sick and infirm. The ministry of Jesus was one of words as well as deeds.

In the gospel, Matthew presents Jesus as beginning his ministry, preaching about reforming one's life since the elusive kingdom is at hand. He gathers his followers to assist and carry on this ministry, and went about curing the people of every kind of illness and disease. The fact that he began this mission outside the confinement of established Jewish circles is an important stylistic device, for through it Matthew indicates that Jesus is the Messiah for all nations.

The Isaian reading coincides with the gospel for it also indicates that those in Galilee, here called the Gentiles, will also experience a light to come into the darkness of their lives, and from this light all the world will come to believe.

The responsorial psalm gives the theme of the liturgy, for the Lord alone is proclaimed as our light and salvation. From him alone comes healing as well as wisdom.

The second theme of the liturgy is from the second reading from First Corinthians. The appeal of Paul is for unity since the church at Corinth was experiencing the deep wounds caused by dissension. This characteristic of Corinth is the same for almost any other church since then. How to make cliques expand into a genuine community, how to encourage dominant personalities to discover that the not-so-dominant have a voice as well, and how to encourage those who pick and choose parts of the Gospel to suit their own needs to open themselves to the entire Gospel is a constant ministry.

Since this reading appears near the week of prayer for Christian unity, it may provide an excellent occasion to preach on the still disunited Christian church. Effective ecumenism comes not by decrees from the central offices of administration, but in the experience of local congregations who begin to work on common purposes and needs.

The prayers of the Sacramentary reflect general themes of the eucharist in the prayer over the gifts and the prayer after communion where we pray that the salvation offered us in the eucharist may bring us salvation, and a share in the joy of the kingdom.

The opening prayer reflects the unity and peace theme of the second reading and the alternate form of the opening prayer speaks of the light and vision of the glory of God which the community experiences at the eucharist.

The chosen preface from among those ordinary Sundays could be number I, about the darkness/light theme mentioned at its conclusion, or number V, about the marvels of the power and wisdom of God, as exemplified in the words and deeds of Jesus.

The prayer over the people could be number 7, about the light that has come to the community from this eucharist.

Guidelines for the celebrant's introduction and comments:

INTRODUCTION

Because of the variety of themes presented in the liturgy the celebrant should compose this to tie in with the theme he wishes to emphasize in the homily. The week of prayer for Christian unity may be part of the introduction as seen in the second reading, or some aspect of the preaching and healing of Jesus in the gospel may need emphasis. If the theme of unity is chosen, the invocations from number IV of the penitential rite should be used; if the theme of Christ as the light and healer is selected, number V of the invocations about his ministry should be used.

BEFORE THE EUCHARISTIC PRAYER

In our prayer of praise and thanksgiving we pray that we may be healed of our disunity and dissensions by this eucharist, a symbol of the unity and peace of the kingdom of God.

BEFORE THE SIGN OF PEACE

May it be a true sign that we will work for the unity that breaks cliques and makes them true communities, and the kind of peace that is based on mutual respect. Let us offer each other a sign of the peace of Christ.

FOURTH SUNDAY IN ORDINARY TIME

The message of the Scripture readings in the liturgy of this Sunday is that the believer is uncomfortable in the world in which he lives. The Gospel does not endorse the *status quo*, and does not find pleasure in keeping things the way they are. Instead, we are faced with contradictions; what we are invited to call the wisdom of God is more often than not called foolishness by this world; what is believed to be God's favor is glibly dismissed as pie-in-the-sky; and the blessings which God bestows on the lowly would more likely be curses on the deprived. The statements of the Sermon on the Mount require critical reflection in the life of the believer to discern where his values lie, and true principles rest.

St. Matthew has stylized the blessing statements of Jesus by casting them in the form of a discourse of the Master as he sits on the side of a mountain. In Jewish circles the mention of giving any teaching on a mountain would immediately conjure up significant recollections of the giving of the Torah to Moses on Sinai. Jesus now transcends this Law and gives another, but it is the setting of the scene as much as it is the statements themselves which indicates that something most important is taking place, even something which would replace the former Law. Jesus teaches from the sitting position which itself indicates prominence and significance for this was a sign and mark of respect for the Jewish teachers.

The nine groups of people exalted by Jesus would not be the most blessed by society since they include the poor in spirit (as well as the poor in fact), those mourning, the meek, those who show mercy, who are peacemakers, and the final and ultimate blessing is that given to those who suffer insult and persecution for the sake of their profession of faith.

The Old Testament lesson from Zephaniah was selected to correspond to the teaching of the sermon, especially with its concentration on the humble who are exalted in the first beatitude.

The responsorial psalm takes the same first beatitude and makes it the response to the psalm, giving priority to the first blessing of the nine.

While the second reading is part of the continuous reading of the First Corinthians, it does link up with the other two lessons since it extends the contradiction of the demands of Jesus to include his wisdom as opposed to the wisdom of the world surrounding the believer. The only boasting for those called by God is to boast in the Lord; for the man of God this is his only wisdom; for the man of the world this is only foolishness. The issue in the readings is who are the "haves" and the "have-nots," the "privileged" and the "underprivileged." More importantly, how does one decide the difference between the two, according to whose wisdom?

The prayers of the Sacramentary are of a general eucharistic theme with the prayer over the gifts and the prayer after communion asking that this sacrament of salvation may help us attain salvation and continued growth in faith.

The opening prayer has a reference to the readings only insofar as they speak of loving others the way God loves them, and in the alternate form, that God has formed us into a community in the image of his Son.

The preface for the Sundays of the year, number II, about Jesus humbling himself and number VIII, about calling the community to be his people to praise his wisdom, as opposed to the wisdom of the world, would seem most appropriate.

The prayer over the people should be number 4, that this community find its fulfillment in God alone, the source of all their hope and longing.

Guidelines for the celebrant's introduction and comments:

INTRODUCTION

My brothers and sisters, we come to share this eucharist to have our vision clarified and our perspective sharpened by the word of God. The values of the Gospel are most often in contradiction with the accepted morality of our society. Let us pause and pray that the word of God truly penetrate our hearts and remake us into a people dedicated to the word and will of God.

PENITENTIAL RITE

Lord Jesus, you exalted the poor and lowly: Lord, have mercy . . .

Lord Jesus, you blessed the peacemakers in this world: Christ, have mercy . . .

Lord Jesus, you bless those who strive to be holy: Lord, have mercy . . .

BEFORE THE READINGS

In the eyes of the world, to be empty and poor is to be among the despised of men. To be empty and poor for Christ are values which the Scripture readings present for our consideration and prayer.

BEFORE THE EUCHARISTIC PRAYER

In place of using the prefaces for the Sundays of Ordinary Time and the eucharistic prayer, the celebrant might choose the fourth prayer with its own preface and emphasize in his introduction to the contradiction in the prayer that Jesus' ministry was to the poor, prisoners, and those in sorrow.

FIFTH SUNDAY IN ORDINARY TIME

Since the time of the Reformation, the debate over "faith" and "good works" as essential for salvation has continued to occupy the attention of believers. What has been at stake most often, however, is a misguided emphasis on the one to the exclusion of the other. To emphasize the letters of Paul to the Romans and Galatians about faith alone bringing justification, or to isolate the saying in the Letter of James about faith being dead without good works, is to do an injustice to the revelation of the whole New Testament. The readings of this Sunday serve to provide a proper proportion and perspective in this debate as the believer has no choice but to show he is "salt" and "light."

The first reading is used in a longer version on the Friday after Ash Wednesday where fasting leads to works of charity and regard for the poor, and is not isolated by itself for the sake of self-discipline. The verses of this Sunday's lesson have a different shade of meaning since they emphasize sharing with the poor and the necessity for men of the darkness to see the work of those who believe in the light and who manifest who they are by their actions. Fasting for show (cf. Matthew 6:1-6, 16-18) is to be replaced by fasting so the goods of the earth may be shared by those in need.

The responsorial psalm speaks of the just man as light, a verse that successfully links the Old Testament with the gospel of the day. Just as Christ shone as a light in the darkness of this world, so the believer now shines as a light to those in the darkness of oppression and physical need. The elements of "salt" and "light" are carefully selected since each enhances another substance; neither dominates that to which it is applied. A true disciple who is faithful to both stands humbly and ready to enhance others; he does not stand aside and dwell on his gifts as possessions. To have the faith in justification means to show the faith in works of sanctification; to show forth good works for the Christian means that he believes in a God who calls him to be a light for others.

The alternate theme of the readings is from the second lesson from Paul's first letter to the Corinthians. The true paradox of Christianity is that by the cross of suffering and death men have been freed from sin and share a new kind of life with God. The scandal of Christianity is the scandal of the cross.

The prayers of the Sacramentary speak in general terms of the eucharist and the only specific application to the readings is found in the prayer after communion which asks that the believers help bring salvation to the world, and in the alternate form of the opening prayer, which uses the language of the sermon on the mount about beatitude for the poor in spirit (more appropriate for the previous Sunday).

The selection of Sunday Preface I, about the characteristics of the community which has been called out of darkness into the light of Christ can help expand the theme of the Old Testament and gospel readings; the use of Sunday Preface II would help amplify the theme of the second reading about the paradox of Jesus' birth from a virgin mother and that his suffering on a cross brought life to the world.

Number 7 of the prayers over the people reflects the main theme of the readings about salt and light; number 17 of these prayers speaks about the necessity of the cross of Christ to bring salvation.

Guidelines for the celebrant's introduction and comments:

INTRODUCTION

My brothers and sisters in Christ, we have come here this Sunday to proclaim and nourish our common faith. We have left the "world" and the "city" (town, village, etc.) in which we live to celebrate this eucharist and to consider the demands which the word of God places upon us as we seek to live our faith not in isolation from, but amid the complexity of the world. The readings we shall hear today speak of us believers in terms of salt and light for the world. Let us pause and pray that we may become fit examples of the light of Christ throughout this coming week.

PENITENTIAL RITE

You are the light of the world: Lord, have mercy . . .

You endured death on a cross that we may live: Christ, have mercy . . .

You call us this day to be salt for the earth: Lord, have mercy . . .

BEFORE THE READINGS

The word of God revealed to us in these readings invites us to a charity that is practical, not put on; and a concern that is sincere, not affected.

BEFORE THE EUCHARISTIC PRAYER

We gather around this altar to experience the vision of the light of Christ and to share in this eucharist that we ourselves might become a light for the darkness of our world.

SIXTH SUNDAY IN ORDINARY TIME

The Old Testament readings, the responsorial psalm, and the gospel for this Sunday taken together might offer simple choices but not simplistic solutions. The gospel reading is from the sermon on the mount and contains the clear statement of Jesus that no part of the Law will be done away with, and that he has not come to do away with any part of the Law and the prophets. The beatitudes clearly state who is blessed and who is not, and the distinction is quite clear.

In the Old Testament reading from Sirach, man is free to choose between fire and water; between life and death; to abide by or not to abide by the commandments of God.

The responsorial psalm reinforces this teaching by exalting the law of the Lord, the precepts which are to be kept diligently.

With this as a setting, the long form of the gospel contains three of the antitheses in the sermon on the mount for man's choice and decision. Jesus here sharpens the Law's demands, for his task was to bring the Law to completion. The Old Law is placed first with the demand of the New Law to complete the former teaching. The instruction about murder now includes anger; the demand about adultery now includes lustful looks; and the demand about false oaths now includes not making any oaths at all. Simple choices, or so it seems, is the regulation of the New Law. Yet, when Jesus becomes specific he cuts even deeper and causes these simple answers to become clouded in complexity. The elaboration of the command about murder and anger gives the specific case of coming for worship and there discovering a break with another. The teaching is not that we have initiated a fight or have a problem with another, but whether or not anyone has anything against us. For this reason, we must leave our gift and first be reconciled, and then return for a proper act of worship. The simple theory becomes clouded practice, and the solution is complex because it affects the lives of each of us as no one of us can say that we are above such a penetrating requirement for pure worship.

Simplistic solutions do not come as the result of the morality of Jesus because no one of us can say that our motives are always the best, our reasons for doing things always single-hearted. The theory is obvious, but the solutions and resolutions take a lifetime. The answer is that these demands of Jesus for a "better righteousness" cannot be achieved by man alone. He needs and always will need God's saving grace to fulfill God's deliberately difficult morality. Christianity is not a matter of will training, but of reliance on the grace of God and our conformity to that grace. We are not left to our own devices to withstand temptations; we are given the grace and peace of God our Father through the same Jesus who reveals the "new" Law.

The alternate theme of the readings is the continuation of First Corinthians about the wisdom of God and the wisdom of man. Here, Paul does admit wisdom on man's part, and in order that this not be misunderstood as a contradiction to last week's reading, reference should be made to both readings in the preacher's homily.

The opening prayer of the liturgy points to the decisions called for in the gospel and Old Testament readings about doing what is right and just. The alternative form ties in with the wisdom theme of the epistle reading as it too speaks of the wisdom of God taking flesh in the person of Jesus Christ.

The prayer over the gifts speaks of obedience to the word of God and can refer either to the morality of the gospel reading or the wisdom of God in the second.

The main theme of the readings finds adequate expression in preface number VII in Christ as a model for all believers and in number 2 of the prayers over the people as well as number 6, about greater fidelity to his commands.

The only oblique reference in a preface to reflect the alternate theme of the readings is number VIII, about praise for the wisdom of God in all his works.

Guidelines for the celebrant's introduction and comments:

INTRODUCTION

My friends, we live in a world which proclaims a "new morality" and ever changing standards of conduct. We gather today as believers in the word of God which this day concerns the morality Jesus came to teach. May we now prepare to open our hearts to measure our lives according to his moral teaching and his moral values.

PENITENTIAL RITE

You came to teach us the Father's will: Lord, have mercy . . .

You invite us to follow your way on earth: Christ, have mercy . . .

You guide our lives by your mercy and your grace: Lord, have mercy . . .

BEFORE THE READINGS

The gift of free will often means that men will follow evil and the wickedness of this world rather than the way of goodness and truth. Today's readings inform us that morality involves a continual struggle of choosing good over evil.

BEFORE THE EUCHARISTIC PRAYER

The difference between Christianity and a philosophical system of beliefs is that in faith we are given the grace of God to sustain us in living his way of life. We come to this altar of sacrifice and nourishment to receive the strength and life of Christ we need to live the demands which his Gospel places upon us.

SEVENTH SUNDAY IN ORDINARY TIME

In discussions about the imitation of Christ and the keeping of the word of God, expressions such as "heroic sanctity" and "extraordinary faith" often characterize the believer. The point of the readings from the holiness code of Leviticus of the Old Testament and the last of the antitheses of the sermon on the mount of the Gospel of St. Matthew indicate in no uncertain terms that sanctity is heroic and faith must be extraordinary. In the face of the teaching of Jesus to offer no resistance to injury, to turn the other cheek, to love enemies, and even to pray for one's persecutors, no one can stand secure if left by himself and to his own devices. The kind of self-control envisioned is uncommon and the kind of love required is impractical. The end of the reading is the completion of the entire sermon with the admonition to be perfect as the Father is perfect. But it is this last admonition with its guarantee of the absolute perfection of Jesus and the first reading about the very holiness of God that makes this teaching understandable and even within the reach and possibility of the believer. God's holiness is placed first before a list of prescriptions since the believer can become holy himself only because of his faith in God.

At the celebration of the eucharist, the Christian comes face to face with the transcendence and sanctity of God so that he who is redeemed and sanctified by the eucharist can and must redeem and sanctify the situation in which he lives. Sacraments are encounters with the all-holy, and man's natural response is "Depart from me for I am a sinful man" (Luke 5:8). But the Lord does not depart or retreat; he remains to give the follower the possibility of renewing and living again according to Jesus' teaching. The need to transcend national barriers, political and personal philosophy, the bonds of race, and even religion in order to fulfill the extraordinary kind of love which Jesus came to teach is only possible because he first brought that extraordinary love in his life to his followers. He who shared the very holiness of God from all eternity came to be one of us that we who know sin might come to know redemption and holiness through him. For this reason communities gather weekly to renew and deepen their own experience of the holiness of God.

The alternate scriptural theme is taken from the conclusion of Paul's counterattack to the position of the Corinthians that they had better and wiser teachers and philosophers than those who preach the wisdom of Christ. The wisdom of this world is passing; the wisdom of God lasts forever.

The opening prayer of the liturgy speaks of the wisdom and love revealed in Jesus and our desire to imitate him in word and deed. The alternative form has the same theme about faith in the word of God and that our every act may show our share in the life which Jesus offered us. Because both prayers speak of living the faith they are particularly helpful to reflect the theme of the gospel, in which the reference to wisdom coincides with the second reading as well.

The prayer over the gifts speaks of this offering in Spirit and truth which offers man his needed and continued salvation to become a believer with heroic sanctity and extraordinary faith.

The prayer after communion corresponds well with the gospel theme in calling the community to live the example of Christ's love shared at the eucharist.

The preface recalling wisdom is number VIII; preface number VI speaks of the love of God and the gift of the Spirit dwelling in the community. This preface also links the celebration of the eucharist to the lives of the assembly for we share now what we hope to share completely in the kingdom - the food which strengthens us to live the faith. An appropriate prayer over the people to reflect the main scriptural theme is number 2 or number 6.

Guidelines for the celebrant's introduction and comments:

INTRODUCTION

My friends, we gather to celebrate these sacred mysteries as a memorial of the new life we share through the redemption of Christ. We come to this table of the word of God to learn of his holiness and love for us and to the table of the eucharist to share in that holiness even now in our lives on earth. Let us reflect on the love of God poured out for us at this celebration of the eucharist.

PENITENTIAL RITE

Lord Jesus, you are the eternal Son of the Father: Lord, have mercy . . .

Lord Jesus, you came to reconcile us with the Father: Christ, have mercy . . .

Lord Jesus, you are the image of the unseen God: Lord, have mercy . . .

BEFORE THE READINGS

Often we regard sanctity as something for someone else, and holiness for other people. In today's readings we are reminded that sanctity and growing in holiness are vocations for each of us since the very holiness of God is made manifest to us in God's word and the eucharist of his Son's body and blood.

BEFORE THE EUCHARISTIC PRAYER

We pray that this our sacrifice of praise and thanksgiving make us worthy sharers in the redemption Christ came to give us. As we offer our praise and thanksgiving may we dedicate ourselves as well to living the holiness we share at this table of the Lord.

EIGHTH SUNDAY IN ORDINARY TIME

Because of the revival of interest in biblical studies and recent developments in the explanation and understanding of the sacraments, the word *covenant* has become an important word in our religious vocabulary. The covenants of the Old Testament between Yahweh and Noah, Abraham, and Moses, as well as the "new covenant" promised in Jeremiah 31:31-34 and inaugurated in the ministry of Jesus form a major part of contemporary catechetical emphasis and teaching.

The personal covenant of the believer and God begins at the sacrament of baptism for in it God takes the initiative and welcomes the person into the community of faith. In the sacrament of the eucharist, that covenant is renewed and developed through the preaching of the word of God and the reception of the sacrament of the Lord's body and blood. The sacrament of marriage is a covenant of mutual and lasting fidelity by which a man and wife join themselves and commit themselves to respond in their covenant of love to God's love for them.

But in none of the biblical covenants is there the aspect of contract, equal partnership, or mutuality between God and his people. There is no equality with God, only a realization that his love and fidelity will far outlast ours; his act of graciousness can never be outdone or even matched by that of man.

The covenant with the people of Israel is the basis for the first reading from Isaiah and it indicates in a very brief fashion that despite man's infidelity, God will be ever faithful. In the book of the prophet Hosea the adulterous spouse and the faithful husband provide ample imagery for the author to cite faithless Israel searching after other gods, and yet in spite of this, Yahweh is faithful and forgiving. The imagery of this reading is family-oriented as well for in the Judaism of that time to break with the family was to break these ties irrevocably. With Yahweh, however, no break is irrevocable, no breach of contract is ever a break of the covenant, no error is an everlasting separation.

The gospel reading from Matthew is filled with examples of the care which God the Father has and shows for his people, for in it the model of family unity and the care of a father for his children is the example of the love of the heavenly Father for his children. By baptism man is made free; free from attachments and undue concern about the things of the world; free to serve God by responding to the love of God in love of neighbor. The application of these readings to the eucharist is obvious for at this sacred banquet man is again brought close to the source of all good things, the source of all grace and blessing.

The alternate theme of the liturgy is from the conclusion of Paul's discourse on factionalism in the Corinthian community. Here he explains that picking and choosing a preacher is to misunderstand the preacher's role and task. It is not the personality of the preacher that is important, but that he preach Christ crucified; it is not the person of the minister of God's word who is important, but the Word to which he ministers. The role is one of service and dedication by his own words and his example.

The opening prayer of the liturgy speaks of the freedom which belongs to those who share in the covenant of God. The alternate prayer is about the peace of Christ and witnessing to the gospel.

The prayer over the gifts and the prayer after communion both speak of the eucharist as a foretaste of the fulfillment of the covenant in the kingdom.

Preface number I and number VIII for Sundays in ordinary time are appropriate selections since they both speak of the covenanted people of God who are holy and are the very body of Christ. A most appropriate alternate for the preface and eucharistic prayer would be to use the fourth eucharistic prayer and its own preface because of the section on the covenant and God's fidelity even when man disobeyed him and lost his friendship.

For the prayer over the people, number 6, about blessing the people even when they stray, and number 24, about blessing those who put their faith in God and who need his strength, are most appropriate.

Guidelines for the celebrant's introduction and comments:

INTRODUCTION

My brothers and sisters, we come together to share this eucharist as members and fellow sharers in the covenant to which God has called us by the sacrament of baptism. This eucharist is our renewal of that covenant and by it we deepen our commitment to live according to God's plan and promises. As we celebrate these sacred mysteries may we grow in our love for our Savior by our love for each other.

PENITENTIAL RITE

Lord Jesus you called us out of darkness to share in your light: Lord, have mercy . . .

Lord Jesus you are the son of the everlasting Father: Christ, have mercy . . .

Lord Jesus you strengthen us by this sacrament of your body and blood: Lord, have mercy . . .

BEFORE THE READINGS

In our world of business partnerships and signed contracts, the idea of a covenant between God and believers can often have the wrong associations. Today's readings reveal to us that this covenant is not among equals, but rather depends solely on God's infinite love for man.

BEFORE THE EUCHARISTIC PRAYER

We now pray that by this sacrament of the body and blood of the Lord we may grow in our response to God's love for us by our love for each other.

NINTH SUNDAY IN ORDINARY TIME

One of the characteristics of the evangelist Matthew is the catechetical orientation of his gospel since he provides illustrations and examples for the lessons he teaches. The gospel reading for this Sunday contains the dominant Matthean theme of showing belief in deeds as well as words, in action as well as theory, in the life a believer leads as well as in what he knows about the faith. The point at issue is the integrity of the believer and the extent to which his actions reflect the words of faith he speaks. It is not those who *say* "Lord, Lord" who will enter the kingdom; it is they who *live* by the word of the Lord. The believer whose faith is consistent both in words and deeds is the man whose integrity of faith is to be respected.

The same theme is reflected in Matthew 19:16-22 when the rich young man knew the commandments and kept them, yet when

Jesus asked that his passive submission become an active commitment he was unable to follow Jesus.

In Matthew 21:28-31 the man who had two sons asked them for help; the first refused, yet ultimately did the task, while the second readily agreed yet did not keep his word. The lesson here is that the first man was the faithful one because he ultimately performed what was asked of him. Actions speak louder than words. The Old Testament lesson from Deuteronomy coincides with this gospel since it speaks of choices in the life of a believer: to choose God's commandments and thereby incur a blessing, or to choose other gods and incur a curse.

The alternative theme is justification by faith alone in the second reading from Romans where the emphasis is on the sacrifice of Jesus and that our redemption is from that one perfect act of love.

The opening prayer and the prayer over the gifts speak in general terms about the eucharist, but the prayer after communion does carry through the theme of the Old Testament and gospel readings by asking that this community may live their faith by the lives they lead, not only by the words they speak. Sunday preface number VII, about the example of the obedience of Christ doing the will of his Father would be most appropriate.

Of the prayers over the people, number 2, about our love for each other and number 11, about doing God's will reflect this same theme.

For the theme from Romans about justification by faith, the alternative wording of the opening prayer about an increase in faith is appropriate.

Sunday preface number VI, about the paschal mystery, the heart of the faith, and number 9 and number 24, of the prayers over the people about belief in God and putting one's trust in God also carry through the theme of the Epistle to the Romans.

Guidelines for the celebrant's introduction and comments:

INTRODUCTION

My brothers and sisters, we come together at this eucharist to choose again to live according to the commands of God as well as to call on him by speaking our common faith. Let us pray at this eucharist that we will reflect in our lives the faith that we proclaim here this day.

PENITENTIAL RITE

Lord Jesus, you were the obedient Son of the Father: Lord, have mercy . . .

Lord Jesus, you reveal to us the will of the Father: Christ, have mercy . . .

Lord Jesus, you nourish and sustain our lives of faith by this eucharist: Lord, have mercy . . .

BEFORE THE READINGS

We have all heard the cliché "actions speak louder than words." Today's readings tell us that speaking our faith in our lives is as important as speaking faith by words.

BEFORE THE EUCHARISTIC PRAYER

As we come to this table of God's grace, mercy, and love, we pray that the obedience of Christ to his Father's will may be an example to us of the obedience that is possible for us who believe in the strength and grace of this sacrament.

TENTH SUNDAY IN ORDINARY TIME

To the Hebrew mentality reflected in the Scriptures, reality consisted in a succession of extremes and opposites where nuances or shades of meaning were almost totally lost because of the very structure of the language. The first reading for this Sunday from the book of Hosea is a prime example since the prophet is concerned about the priority of mercy along with a proper understanding and performance of ritual sacrifice. Hosea does not want rituals abandoned, he wants them purified and properly used, not mindlessly and perfunctorily abused. Crude ideas about sacrifice need reforming, but man still needs the ritual of sacrifice.

The last line of this first reading forms the conclusion to the day's gospel and, therefore, was selected to introduce it; and it is in the gospel that the need of man for the table-fellowship with the Lord is emphasized. For Matthew it is important that Jesus eats with sinners to heal and strengthen them; it is in Matthew 9:2-8 that the paralytic is healed by the pronouncement of forgiveness by Jesus; it is in Matthew's Last Supper account alone that we find the reference to the cup of salvation for the forgiveness of sins. Man stands in need of the sacrifice of the eucharist to forgive his sins and strengthen him in his Christian life. The image of God in the gospel is a Lord of mercy, forgiveness, and love who saves us despite our human weaknesses, failings, and in fact strengthens us precisely because of our weakness, cleanses us because of our failings, and raises our human life to touch all that is divine in him. Hosea the prophet and Matthew the evangelist do not ask for sacrifices and rituals to hide behind; they want the chosen people to share in God's love at their liturgical celebrations, until the day when "sacraments will cease" and the pilgrim church becomes the assembly of the elect who share eternal table-fellowship with the heavenly Father. This theme finds expression in the language of many prayers over the gifts for they often speak of the forgiveness of sins as one of the reasons for the celebration of the eucharist.

The alternate theme for this Sunday is taken from the reading from Romans with the concrete example of Abraham as the man of faith. The trust of this man was extraordinary since the promise that he would become the father of many nations beginning at his age of one hundred was beyond human expectation and the natural course of events. The quality of faith more often than not involves trust in seeming contradictions.

In the prayers for this Sunday, the alternate opening prayer speaks of the love of God for man through Jesus. That we all are to grow in that love is the prayer over the gifts, and that the eucharist is a sacrament of the healing love of God is the prayer after communion.

Sunday preface number III, about salvation through Christ, or number VI, about the eucharist as a promise and foretaste of the paschal feast of heaven are appropriate selections.

The prayer over the people number 3, about cherishing the gifts of the eucharist, number 5, about the strength believers receive from the eucharist or number 18, about the eucharist as a pledge of continual rebirth leading to new life with God are appropriate.

For the theme of the faith of Abraham, Sunday preface number VI proclaiming the paschal mystery as the core of the faith is suitable, and number 1 of the prayers over the people speaks clearly of God's initiative in calling us to faith.

Guidelines for the celebrant's introduction and comments:

INTRODUCTION

My friends, we gather this day to experience the grace and mercy and love of God for us as his pilgrim Church on earth. We come to share an experience of his presence, not merely to perform an exercise in external piety. May a moment of silence serve to remind us that our celebration of these sacred mysteries demands our attention and participation in faith.

PENITENTIAL RITE

You ate with sinners to grant them your forgiveness: Lord, have mercy . . .

You came to free us from our sins and failures: Christ, have mercy . . .

You come to offer us your healing and your strength: Lord, have mercy . . .

BEFORE THE READINGS

Sacraments and religious rituals were made for man's sanctification and redemption; yet they can easily become mindless exterior practices. The readings in this liturgy invite us to reflect on the quality of our faith and devotion at the table of the Lord.

BEFORE THE EUCHARISTIC PRAYER

We come before this table of God's grace and forgiveness the way sinners ate with Jesus in today's gospel. May we appreciate the presence of our Savior and Lord who comes to free us from our sins, and to remake us according to his image and likeness.

ELEVENTH SUNDAY IN ORDINARY TIME

The doctrine of election is a difficult concept to present adequately and without prejudice. A poor presentation of election can lead to unfortunate consequences where this scripturally based doctrine becomes a source of bias and exclusivism. The refrain of the responsorial psalm, "we are his people the sheep of his flock," reflects the theme of both the Old Testament and the gospel readings for we are a people chosen to do his will—a will that compels us to missionary concerns, not self-satisfaction in being elected. The reading from Exodus is a preliminary to the Sinai covenant where Israel is dearer to Yahweh than any other nation; Israel is to become a kingdom of priests, a holy nation. They needed to grow in holiness and to become a mission-oriented group rather than remain a self-contained body. Israel was specially chosen and enjoyed God's favor, but that election was not to mean isolation and self-satisfaction.

The gospel of the day contains the summons of Jesus to the apostles to proclaim the imminence of the reign of God. It is only here at their commissioning that Matthew gives the names of the

Twelve, not at their "election." This stylistic change from the other synoptics indicates Matthew's stance in favor of sending forth the apostles rather than allowing them to keep the news of the kingdom to themselves. The statement at the end of this pericope about preaching first to the lost sheep of the house of Israel should not be taken to mean exclusivism toward the original elected people, for at the end of this gospel (Matthew 28:16-21), Jesus commands the apostles to make disciples of *all* nations. Furthermore, the command to preach the coming of the reign of God is not a clerical preserve, for the same command belongs to the entire people of God, "a chosen race, a royal priesthood, a holy nation, God's own people," since it is everywhere that we are to proclaim his mighty works (from Sunday Preface I). The biblical doctrine of election invites critical reflection on the extent to which we have evangelized the world or kept the Gospel to an isolated band of elite. Both can be interpreted as results of election; only the first is faithful to the Scripture readings of this Sunday.

The alternate theme of the second reading is about justification, mediation, and the end of our estrangement from God through Christ Jesus. We were redeemed, while we were still sinners, because of God's act of love in the death of Jesus on a cross. It is through the sinless one that we have access to the Father, whom we worship at the eucharist, "through Christ our Lord."

The alternative version of the opening prayer cites the problem of selfishness on the part of the Church and indicates from the outset the major theme of the day's readings. Sunday Preface number I or VIII both speak of the body of Christ and the vocation of this chosen people.

Of the prayers over the people, number 9 and number 23 speak of the gift of God's love for this community and the task which this community has to share that love with others. For the theme of the meditation of God's love through Christ from the Epistle to the Romans, Sunday Preface VII, about the disobedience of man and redemption through the obedience of Christ, would be the best selection; and number 5 of the prayers over the people, about being faithful to the Lord and rejoicing in God's mercy, is a fitting blessing.

Guidelines for the celebrant's introduction and comments:

INTRODUCTION

My friends, we gather this day as members of the chosen people of God. Yet, we are reminded in today's readings that to be chosen means to be sent forth to preach the good news of Christ to others. May we pray at this eucharist for the grace we need to share our faith with others and not to rest secure in keeping it to ourselves.

PENITENTIAL RITE

Lord Jesus, you reconciled mankind to your Father: Lord, have mercy . . .

Lord Jesus, you have called us to be your chosen people: Christ, have mercy . . .

Lord Jesus, you call us this day to be your witnesses in this world: Lord, have mercy . . .

BEFORE THE READINGS

An ever-present temptation of the Church is to become isolated and removed from the concerns of the rest of mankind. Today's readings remind us that to be God's chosen people means that each of us is called to preach and teach others the good news of the salvation we have received.

BEFORE THE EUCHARISTIC PRAYER

The summons we have received in God's word this day is to grow in holiness and mission. May we who draw near to the Lord in this eucharist become the very holiness of God and witness to his word.

TWELFTH SUNDAY IN ORDINARY TIME

The call to be a prophet of God's word, to transmit to men his message in a given circumstance and to be sent forth to preach and teach the Gospel has an enduring appeal and a certain romantic flavor. Yet, the Scripture readings of this Sunday indicate that such a commission is necessarily unpopular and will involve suffering and humiliation for the one sent forth.

The reading from Jeremiah has the tone and force of a lamentation psalm where persecutors are all around the just man, and his only strength is the Lord himself.

The gospel speaks as well of the persecution that the apostles will have to endure as they preach the good news of Jesus where their only security is the knowledge of the presence of God with them. That the Son of Man had to suffer and die to bring redemption to all men means that his followers too will have to endure persecution for the sake of the Gospel. There is no smooth progression from the event of Easter to the eschaton, and in the meantime, the pilgrim Chruch will be persecuted for the sake of the preaching of the Gospel.

The alternate theme of the second reading involves an increasingly important question theologically and pastorally—the biblical doctrine of original sin and redemption. The typology is of Adam and Christ, the fall and redemption, sin and eternal life. A clear presentation of the statements here about the second Adam freeing mankind from the heritage left to the descendants of the first Adam can have great value pastorally since the understanding of original sin and justification could use a solid biblical foundation in most congregations.

The alternative version of the opening prayer speaks indirectly of the persecution believers will have to endure as the contrast is between the uncertainty of this world and the Lord's faithful covenant.

Sunday Preface II about the humility and suffering of Jesus, is an appropriate selection since it presents the model for that which the Church will experience throughout her lifetime on earth.

Of the prayers over the people, number 5, about remaining faithful to the Lord, and number 7, about the suffering and agony of the cross, are equally suited to the message of the readings.

For the theme of the Adam/Christ typology, the prayer after communion assures the community of the redemption of Christ as it is experienced in the eucharist. Of the Sunday prefaces, number III, about salvation through Christ despite man's refusal of God's friendship, number VII, about man's disobedience and Christ's obedience, or number VIII, about our sin and Christ's redemption, are all appropriate options.

Of the prayers over the people, number 14, about the mystery of redemption reflects again this theme of lost innocence and redemption.

Guidelines for the celebrant's introduction and comments:

INTRODUCTION

My brothers and sisters, we gather together as a people who must necessarily endure suffering and rejection because of our affirmation and lives of faith. Each of us is called to be the prophetic voice of God who speaks to our society of his ways, not man's. May we who must endure suffering for our faith enjoy the faithful presence of God in our midst at this eucharist.

PENITENTIAL RITE

You came to reunite us with the Father: Lord, have mercy . . .

You came to teach us the will of the Father: Christ, have mercy . . .

You are present with us this day as the sacrament of the Father's love: Lord, have mercy . . .

BEFORE THE READINGS

The call to be a prophet or witness to God's truth contains its romantic aspects as well as its moments of rejection. Today's readings invite us to consider that our position of being believers in this world necessarily involves suffering for the sake of the name of Jesus.

BEFORE THE EUCHARISTIC PRAYER

The body and blood of Christ is poured out at this altar for our consolation and redemption. May we be strengthened by the sharing of this one bread and one cup in our vocation to witness to the truth of the Gospel in our changing world.

THIRTEENTH SUNDAY IN ORDINARY TIME

From the visits of the holy man Elisha to the house of the Shunmite woman (first reading), to the command of Jesus to receive prophets and holy men (gospel reading), to the custom of the early Christians to share all things in common (Acts 2:42-46), and the admonition of Paul to make hospitality our special concern (Romans 12:13), the practice of generosity and hospitality has been one of the marks of the believing Church. Even the Rule of St. Benedict instructs the monks in the most cloistered and remote settings to receive all guests as Christ. The sight of Christians loving each other begins in charity of the most practical sort, in opening one's house to others. The message of the gospel contains three instructions: to leave family and friends for the sake of preaching the gospel ("let goods and kindred go, this mortal life also" of "A Mighty Fortress"), to take up one's personal cross for the sake of preaching the cross of Christ, and to welcome strangers and preachers as the very person of Christ. It is this last instruction which receives priority this Sunday since the Old Testament lesson concerns the hospitality offered to Elisha when he visited the region of Shunem. A further dimension is added to the openhouse of the first reading since the context of the Matthean instruction is the missionary discourse of Jesus. To welcome a prophet is to welcome the very presence of God, and to welcome the prophet's word is to welcome the word of God as well. The identification of the prophet with him who sent him forth, and the holy man with the holiness of God is a significant scriptural theme. The cutting edge of this gospel is not how well do congregations entertain their preachers, but how well they welcome the word of God that preachers direct to them. Hospitality means a welcoming of the word of God into the homes and hearts of believers.

The alternate theme of this Sunday is the classic baptismal text of the Easter Vigil and the revised funeral liturgy, chapter 6 of the Epistle to the Romans. The point at issue here is the quality of the lives of the believers who share God's life through the waters of baptism. The passage from death to life demands a continual passing over from one's former way of life and orientation to life lived according to the baptism we have received.

The alternative form of the opening prayer speaks of God's truth and forming the lives of the community according to truth and love.

The prayer over the gifts asks that those who share in the eucharist will also be faithful servants of the Lord.

Sunday Preface number VIII, about the characteristics of the Church as the body of Christ and the dwelling place of the Spirit, comes closest to the theme of the Scriptures about the qualities of hospitality and generosity of the Church.

Number 12 of the prayers over the people asks that those who receive the eucharist may serve the Lord always, one aspect of which is to welcome the presence of the Lord through the word of God and the ministers.

The regular form of the opening prayer is almost a perfect selection for the reading from Romans 6 as it speaks of the theme of darkness and light, the situation of the believer before and after the regenerative bath of baptism.

Sunday Prefaces number I and number VII are both proper selections to correspond with this theme since the one speaks of sharing the glory of God through the cross and resurrection of his Son, and the other speaks of redemption through the obedience of Christ.

Of the prayers over the people number 4, about avoiding evil as a consequence of baptism and the celebration of the eucharist, and number 7, about sharing Christ's light and devoting oneself to doing God's will, reflect the exhortation and instruction about baptism in the second reading.

Guidelines for the celebrant's introduction and comments:

INTRODUCTION

My brothers and sisters, we gather this day to share in this sacrament of the generosity and love of God through Jesus his Son. We pray that we may be equally generous in responding to his love by sharing it with others in forms of practical charity and hospitality.

PENITENTIAL RITE

You welcomed the hospitality and generosity of many people: Lord, have mercy . . .

You ate with sinners and those who needed mercy: Christ, have mercy . . .

You call us this day to welcome your word and your truth: Lord, have mercy . . .

BEFORE THE READINGS

The incident of hospitality being offered to Elisha leads us to reflect seriously on our obligation to share what we have with those in need even to the point of welcoming them into our own homes. We come to this eucharist to welcome the word of God

Sundays in Ordinary Time

and to allow it to challenge and deepen our lives of Christian faith.

BEFORE THE EUCHARISTIC PRAYER

The Lord sustains us as his people by this sacrament of his body and blood, as well as by the nourishment of his word. May both his word and sacrament this day inspire us to live lives of deeper charity and love for those less fortunate than ourselves.

FOURTEENTH SUNDAY IN ORDINARY TIME

The style and form of the first part of the gospel for this Sunday seems foreign to the design and plan of the synoptic accounts and appears more characteristically Johannine. The long discourses of John 14-17 begin as prayers to the Father in a fashion similar to that found in Matthew 11:25, "Father, I offer praise." Yet, despite the unfamiliar context, the message and appeal to the lonely and mere children is a characteristic of the gospel of Matthew. In the beginning of chapter eighteen he alludes to the incident of Jesus and a little child where the Lord exalts the child's simplicity and declares that only those with a like simplicity could enter the kingdom.

In another context both in Mark and Luke, Jesus uses the example of a child and informs the disciples that those who seek greatness should rather seek the position of a child, the "least" in the eyes of this world. The association of Jesus with the lonely and his ministry involving a simple wisdom are very much to the point of Matthew's Gospel.

The selection of the reading from the prophet Zechariah as the Old Testament lesson indicates that the humility asked for by Jesus is the kind that he himself endured, for he came in meekness and without pageantry, yet his dominion would be to the ends of the earth. The example of the humble servant is the very person of Jesus himself who invites us in the second part of the gospel to come to him for refreshment and rest. This gospel passage is also one of those used at Masses for the dead because this second section provides comfort and hope for those who mourn.

The alternate theme of the Scripture readings is taken from Romans 8 which contains one of the most important yet often misunderstood themes of St. Paul. The hellenistic dichotomy between the lower and higher nature is not found here, for flesh and spirit mean the whole man and the whole man stands in need of redemption by Christ. The Pauline teaching is not that part of man is redeemed and part of him is damnable. Rather man's whole personality is redeemed by the sacrifice of Christ. The vocation of the Christian, both "body" and "soul," is to conform his already redeemed person to the same Spirit he has already received at baptism.

The opening prayer of the liturgy refers to the obedience of Jesus, the servant of the Father, and may be understood as a reference to the example and model of our humility. The proclamation of the fourth eucharistic prayer with its own preface is a proper substitute for the Sunday prefaces, for this prayer clearly emphasized the humility of the Messiah envisioned in the first reading from Zechariah.

The prayer over the people should be number 24 because of the reference to "children" of the faith, and the strength they receive from the eucharist, the sacrament of wisdom and refreshment.

Both forms of the opening prayer refer to the saving power of God in redeeming the fallen world and the alternative version refers specifically to the baptized in that sin will not hinder the redemption they have received.

Sunday Preface number IV which speaks of our identification with the death and resurrection of Jesus and number VI, about our identification with the Father through the Son and the Spirit, are appropriate choices to complete the theme of Romans 8.

Of the prayers over the people, number 20, about filling the community with the love of God, his holiness, and the richness of his grace, reflects the generosity and love of God by which we are saved.

Guidelines for the celebrant's introduction and comments:

INTRODUCTION

My brothers and sisters, we come together to celebrate the redemption Christ won for us by humbling himself to take the form of a servant. May we who celebrate these sacred mysteries conform ourselves to the example of Christ's humility by the power and grace of this sacrament.

PENITENTIAL RITE

You came to live among us as a man: Lord, have mercy . . .

You are forever the Lord, the God of power and might: Christ, have mercy . . .

You are our way to eternal life: Lord, have mercy . . .

BEFORE THE READINGS

One of the basic challenges to understanding the Christian faith is the seeming contradiction of a Messiah who was both God and man, our Lord and a servant. The readings today invite us to deepen our undersatnding of this Messiah who calls us to himself at this eucharist for his grace and peace.

BEFORE THE EUCHARISTIC PRAYER

As we approach the table of the Lord, let us come with the full confidence and assurance that Christ calls us to himself to receive his rest, light, and peace.

FIFTEENTH SUNDAY IN ORDINARY TIME

With the readings for this Sunday the Lectionary presents the beginning of the section of Matthew's Gospel in which Jesus speaks in parables. The roots of this genre of literature can be traced to wisdom and rabbinic literature. They are stories told to convey a religious truth applicable to the lives of the hearers, which force the hearer to a decision about his faith and response to the word of God. There are most often two levels to these parables and illustrations. The first level is the interpretation and application of Jesus in the original form, and the second is the addition of usually allegorical material to the parables by the primitive Church, which reinterpreted the parable to fit its own situations. Such is the ever-present challenge for the proclamation of the Gospel, to take the original story and illustration of Jesus and apply it to the contemporary experience of the community which hears the parable in a culture and society far removed from the world for which it was originally intended.

A fitting introduction to the proclamation of all the parables is the first reading of this Sunday from Deutero-Isaiah. God's ways are not man's ways, and God's word requires a probing analysis by its hearers for it always completes the task it was sent to accomplish; it never returns to the Lord empty. The end in view for the proclamation of the parable from St. Matthew is to cause personal and communal reflection on our response to the word of God and what kind of soil we provide for the flourishing of God's message to man. It is always a two-edged sword, penetrating, demanding and probing the hearts of its hearers. For in hearing the word of God one is engaged in active evaluation and prayer about his own life. Hearing the word is not a passive experience of understanding and information, it is an act of creation and recreating man in God's image and likeness; it involves a continual process of conversion.

The first interpretation of the parable is optimistic, that the reign of God will ultimately triumph despite obstacles in its way. The second interpretation is the explanation of verses 18-23 where there are four types of hearers of the word, three of whom do not really "hear" it at all. The only one who really hears and accepts the challenge of the word is the one who produces a bountiful harvest, (verse 23) and called the "good soil" (verse 8) in Jesus' own interpretation.

The alternate theme of the Scripture readings is the testimony of Paul in Romans 8 about present suffering and the glory of God. Suffering is an essential part of the Christian life and one who truly believes will have his or her share of hardships and trials. Yet, these are not ends in themselves, as there is hope that they will terminate with the full revelation of the glory of God. The theme and message of Paul is not to lose hope in the Lord into whose risen life we have been initiated by baptism.

The opening prayer of the liturgy points to the truth of Christ, which comes from his word and guides us to follow his way. The celebration of the word of God and the proclamation of the eucharist is an invitation to growth in holiness, faith (prayer over the gifts), and love (prayer after communion). Of the Sunday prefaces, no one of them reflects more adequately than the others the theme of the readings of the day, while number 20 of the prayers over the people speaks of the good news of salvation.

Sunday Preface VII about the necessity of Christ's suffering leading to his sharing in the Father's glory and VI, about the eucharist as a pledge of eternal glory with the Father, are equally appropriate selections. Of the prayers over the people, number 4 about the fulfillment of man's longing, and number 16, about present consolation and a promise of the life to come, are proper selections for the final blessing.

Guidelines for the celebrant's introduction and comments:

INTRODUCTION

My friends, we gather at the Sunday celebration of the eucharist to hear God's holy word and receive the sacrament of our redemption. The word of God read for us this day invites us to question our personal response to his word and our willingness to conform ourselves to his truth. May a moment of silence now prepare our minds and hearts for the hearing of God's word.

PENITENTIAL RITE

You are the Word of the Father: Lord, have mercy . . .

Your word is our truth: Christ, have mercy . . .

You are our way to salvation: Lord, have mercy . . .

BEFORE THE READINGS

The word of God has been described as a two-edged sword since at the moment we feel comfortable with one of its edges and feel we have fulfilled its commands, it cuts at us from another direction. Today's readings question our ability to open ourselves to this revelation of God to man.

BEFORE THE EUCHARISTIC PRAYER

As we gather around this table to share the meal of our sanctification, we receive from Christ the grace and strength we need to conform ourselves to the truth of his holy word.

SIXTEENTH SUNDAY IN ORDINARY TIME

The three parables which comprise the long form of the gospel for this Sunday may be termed parables of growth. The point at issue is the growth and expansion of the reign of God from insignificant origins, the size of the proverbially small mustard seed, to wide and significant expanse, the size of a remarkably large tree. The parable of the leaven in the mass of dough also indicates that the reign of God has beginnings that are small when compared to the size of its full stature. The parable of the weeds is also a parable of growth since both weeds and wheat remain until the harvest when they will be divided, the one a pile of good growth, the other of weeds to be burned. Yet, this is not the only message of the parable of the weeds since another aspect concerns judgment as much as the growth of the field. The discerning eye of the harvester is interpreted allegorically by the primitive Christian to mean the judgment of the Son of man as to the quality of the faith of the members of the Church. The context for the judgment is not the customary world-Church division, but rather the unfamiliar and more penetrating judgment within the kingdom of the Son of Man, the Church herself. While the Church must grow and mature into the kingdom of the Father, there are also elements within the faith community which are not in accord with the expansion of the faithful. Weeds as well as wheat, evil men as well as good men, hypocrites as well as the faithful inhabit the Church in Matthew's Gospel. Church membership is no guarantee of salvation or an assurance of joining the elect in the kingdom of the Father. The question is one of integrity and fidelity in following the word of the Lord. This judgment theme is emphasized by the presence of the Old Testament lesson from the Book of Wisdom about judgment, where the author reminds us that the kind of judgment depends not on the scales of the goddess justice, but instead on the mercy and love of God to those who strive to live his life in response to his love.

The comparatively brief reading from Romans provides the second theme of the Scripture readings, the activity of the Spirit in helping us in our weakness to pray as we ought, for it is the Spirit who makes intercession for us and intercedes for us before God.

The alternative opening prayer of the liturgy speaks of the theme of the parable of the wheat and weeds for it asks that God's life may grow in us and also that we may be kept true to Christ's teaching, as a faithful member of his Church. Sunday Preface VIII, about the Church and the body of Christ, corresponds to the teaching that the Church is the community of those eager to conform themselves to Christ and become the dwelling place of the spirit.

Of the prayers over the people, number 2 about remaining faithful to the Lord, number 5, about remaining faithful as well as rejoicing in God's mercy, and number 12, about serving the Lord with all our hearts, all reflect the theme of the parables in the gospel.

The alternative form of the opening prayer also reflects the second theme of the Scripture readings since it asks that the community be kept watchful in prayer, which fidelity depends on the power of the Spirit. Sunday Preface VI, about the Spirit as the foretaste and promise of the paschal feast of heaven, and VIII, about the power and the dwelling place of the Spirit in the Church, continue the reference of Romans to the power of the Spirit helping us in our weakness.

Guidelines for the celebrant's introduction and comments:

INTRODUCTION

My brothers and sisters, we gather at this eucharist to be strengthened in our faith and response to the word of God. Let us pray that we who are gathered in the name of Jesus may be judged worthy members of his kingdom.

PENITENTIAL RITE

You call us to be your holy people: Lord, have mercy . . .

You send us your Spirit to strengthen our faith: Christ, have mercy . . .

You intercede for us at the right hand of the Father: Lord, have mercy . . .

BEFORE THE READINGS

The word of God this Sunday reminds us that we shall be judged by Christ Jesus, not on the grounds of what church we belong to, but by the quality of our faith and the integrity of our living according to his word. Let him who has ears take heed!

BEFORE THE EUCHARISTIC PRAYER

We pray that this eucharist will make us worthy sharers in the kingdom of the Father, a kingdom that is opened for us through the sacrifice of the blood of Christ his Son and our Lord.

SEVENTEENTH SUNDAY IN ORDINARY TIME

The recounting of the parables of the kingdom of God continues this Sunday with the three about the treasure in the field, the pearl of great price, and the dragnet. Structurally the first two belong together and the third resembles the parable of the gospel of the fifteenth Sunday, the parable of the wheat and weeds. Yet, despite the difference between the two types of parables this Sunday, there is an important lesson in their juxtaposition. The man who finds the reign of God is so overjoyed and values his discovery so highly that he sells all that he owns to buy the field that contains the treasure, or he sells all his other possessions to purchase the really valuable pearl.

The moment of the discovery of the kingdom is the moment of the act of conversion in the life of a believer. This moment of discovery never fades, and his priorities and values are forever ordered according to this conversion moment.

The parable of the dragnet containing things which are valuable as well as worthless, where the things of value are kept and the useless things are discarded, is an image of judgment. The first two parables deal with the immanence and presence of the kingdom, whereas the third speaks of waiting until the end of the world when the faithful will be separated from the unfaithful. Like Solomon in the Old Testament reading, we must live according to the wisdom of God to be found among the elect. In the time between becoming a convert and the division of the members of the Church at the end of time, the faithful believer practices discernment and right judgment in choosing things that will aid his life of faith and in avoiding those things that hinder that faith.

The theme of the second reading from the Epistle to the Romans concerns the graciousness and mercy of God at work in calling men to himself, justifying them, and glorifying them as well. The point of the reading is the eternal mystery of the ineffable love of God for man, even before man existed. The use of the term "predestined" can lead to unfortunate misconceptions if the preacher does not refer to later theological opinions and systems. It refers to God's eternal plan of redemption for his people not as individuals, but as members of his body, the Church.

The discernment required of a believer who must await the complete establishment of the kingdom of God is reflected in the opening prayer of the liturgy for it asks that we use wisely the blessings God has given to the world.

The prayer over the gifts contains a plea that we grow in holiness as we await fulfillment of the kingdom and the prayer after communion asks that we be brought closer to eternal salvation by the celebration of the eucharist. Sunday Preface VIII, about the Church as the body of Christ, reflects the imagery of the gospel parables of those awaiting the fulfillment of the kingdom who celebrate in the meantime the saving presence of God in their midst at the eucharist.

Of the prayers over the people, number 2, about remaining faithful to the Lord, number 5, about remaining faithful and rejoicing in God's mercy, and number 12, about serving the Lord with all our hearts, all reflect the theme of the gospel of the day.

The alternative form of the opening prayer speaks of God's love for man at work in creation, and in the life he gives to man, the prayer over the gifts asks that we be made holy by these sacred rites and hence faithful in our lives to the love of God made manifest to us in Christ Jesus.

The infinite love of God for man is reflected in Sunday Preface III as well as in V, but in the latter man's consequent obligations to praise and glorify the Father provide a balance to what could become an over-emphasis on God's love without due regard for man's response.

Of the prayers over the people, number 20, about God's grace, would be the most appropriate to reflect the reading from the Epistle to the Romans.

Guidelines for the celebrant's introduction and comments:

INTRODUCTION

My friends, we assemble on this Lord's day to celebrate the infinite power and love of God who has sent his Son to be our redeemer and who will come again at the end of time to judge the living and the dead. May we who live in the meantime have his wisdom of true discernment to choose those things which will keep us faithful to him.

PENITENTIAL RITE

Lord Jesus, you preached the good news of the kingdom: Lord, have mercy . . .

Lord Jesus, you are the Son of the Most High: Christ, have mercy . . .

Lord Jesus, you will come in glory to judge the living and the dead: Lord, have mercy . . .

BEFORE THE READINGS

The readings today remind us that we are a pilgrim Church—in the world but not at home in it. To live a life according to the wisdom of God is the destiny of all believers. The wisdom granted to Solomon is granted to us this day through the hearing of God's word.

BEFORE THE EUCHARISTIC PRAYER

May we who share the very body and blood of Christ remain faithful to these sacred mysteries all the days of our lives and so be chosen among the faithful and the elect in the kingdom of our heavenly Father.

EIGHTEENTH SUNDAY IN ORDINARY TIME

In today's gospel, the setting of the miraculous distribution of food, the manner of the blessing of the bread, and the association of this reading with the first reading from Deutero-Isaiah are all as important stylistically as the event of the multiplication of the loaves and fish itself. Matthew presents Jesus as the new Moses in the sermon on the mount for he proclaims the will and law of his Father in much the same style and fashion as did Moses at Sinai. In the gospel of the multiplication of the loaves and fishes, Jesus is again the new Moses because he feeds the crowds with bread the way Moses did with manna from heaven. He performs this act after crossing over to a deserted place by boat, a subtle reminder of Moses' crossing the Red Sea to fulfill God's plan to save the Chosen People. Jesus takes the five loaves and two fishes, which are in themselves symbols of the eucharist, and blesses them in such a way that by blessing, breaking, and distributing the loaves he feeds the disciples the way he would feed them again at the Last Supper (Matthew 26:26), the way he continues to nourish and sustain the Church with the food of the eucharist.

The eschatological dimension of the miracle story is provided by the first reading from Deutero-Isaiah, where the banquet for the poor of his time is a promise and a foretaste of what will come in the completed messianic banquet in the kingdom. The table-fellowship of the Lord with sinners and those who need his healing power is renewed for the community of the Church as they gather weekly to break the bread of his word and sacrament until the time when they meet the Lord finally in the kingdom of his Father to share a table-fellowship that is eternal.

The responsorial psalm links the Old Testament and the gospel reading with the present experience of the Church as the Lord continues to feed us at the celebration of the eucharist.

The second theme of the readings is the conclusion of the eighth chapter of Romans where the statement which concludes the reading is the theme of the entire chapter: that nothing can separate us from the love of God through Christ Jesus. The examples Paul uses are principalities, powers, and astrological forces which stand in the way of professing faith, but there are many contemporary examples which would provide adequate re-interpretation of Paul's ideas.

Both the prayer over the gifts and the prayer after communion reflect the eucharist theme of the readings. Of the Sunday prefaces, number VI which refers to the paschal feast of heaven and number VIII, about redemption through the blood of Christ, adequately reflect the scriptural theme of the gospel.

The third eucharistic prayer should be used as it contains the line from the prayer over the gifts, "may he make us an everlasting gift to you."

The prayers over the people which can be interpreted to reflect the event of the feeding of the multitude or the feeding of the Church with the sacrament of the eucharist are numbers 3, 16, 18, 19, and 23.

The opening prayer of the liturgy speaks of the everlasting goodness of the Father and this links with the theme of the reading from Romans about the everlasting love of God through Christ Jesus. Sunday Preface III refers to the Father's loving plan of salvation through Christ, VI speaks of the Father's love through Christ and through the Spirit (a major theme of Romans 8), and VII speaks of sending of God's Son to be our redeemer to show forth the love the Father has for us.

Of the prayers over the people, number 8 speaks of the continuance of God's love for us, and number 17 speaks of the love which Jesus has shown us.

Guidelines for the celebrant's introduction and comments:

INTRODUCTION

My brothers and sisters, the celebration of the eucharist should be understood from the perspective of God's love poured out for us anew through his Son and as man's response to that love in an act of praise, glory, and thanksgiving. As we prepare to offer our act of worship, let us recall the infinite love of God for us through the life and death of his Son.

PENITENTIAL RITE

Lord Jesus, you died and rose for our salvation: Lord, have mercy . . .

Lord Jesus, you are the Lamb of God who takes away our sins: Christ, have mercy . . .

Lord Jesus, you bring us in this life a share in life eternal: Lord, have mercy . . .

BEFORE THE READINGS

The sharing of a common meal has always been a mark of friendliness, concern, and warmth. We who share this eucharist are reminded in these readings that this meal is a sharing in God's love for us and a partaking in the redemption of Christ.

BEFORE THE EUCHARISTIC PRAYER

As we offer this great prayer of glorifying and praising God for his love and care for us, may we realize that his love is ever present for us in the sharing of the sacrifice of his Son, renewed, and poured out again for us at the table of the eucharist.

NINETEENTH SUNDAY IN ORDINARY TIME

There are three important themes present in the gospel for this Sunday: the power of Christ over wind and water, the significant position Peter enjoys in the early Church, and the confession of the confused faith of the apostles in Christ.

The very setting and natural phenomena of the story recall the power of God at creation by separating the water (Genesis), the victory of God in saving the Chosen People from the waters of the Red Sea (Exodus), and the event recorded earlier in Matthew of Christ stilling the storm (Matthew 8:23-27).

The marvel of the apostles that Jesus is the Lord over the wind and sea gives credence to the theory of some commentators who maintain that Christ brings to fulfillment the work of creation begun by his Father. This emphasis on the natural phenomena in the gospel is begun in the reading from 1 Kings about Elijah's experience of the presence of the Lord, who cannot be identified with any natural phenomenon: neither wind, nor earthquake, nor fire, not even the gentle breeze, for the experience of God is of him who is master over all these things. Thus in the gospel, Jesus is acclaimed as the Son of God because of his control over these forces as well.

The prominence of Peter provides another theme for consideration as it is he who emerges to join the Lord, leaving the others behind in the boat, itself an early symbol of the Church of Christ.

But it is the third theme of the instruction of the apostles and their appreciation of the person of Jesus that requires major emphasis. They are to carry out the mission and message of Jesus and are called aside at the beginning of chapter 14 for their own proper ministry. It is they who should have firm faith and confident hope in the presence of God with them. And yet previously in 8:25, they cry out almost in despair for in the storm they fear death, just the way Peter cried out "Lord, save me" in 14:30. The men cry out "Lord," a title of respect and faith proclamation, but the Lord accuses them as well as Peter of having "little faith." The catechetical import and interest of Matthew is apparent here for he wants to convey to those of his present Church and for Christians of future generations, that to have doubts and problems with the faith involves no curse and should not be feared. This was the experience of the primitive community, and the process of making the act of faith again and again by present-day Christians will never be totally completed.

Sundays in Ordinary Time

The theme of the second reading from the Epistle to the Romans sets up the problem the author will deal with in chapters nine through eleven. What is at issue is the lack of faith in Christ as the Messiah on the part of the original Chosen People of God, the Israelites. The anguish and pain Paul endures because they do not believe provides a fitting personal introduction to these chapters in which he deals with the relationship between Jew and Christian in salvation history.

Of the prayers of the liturgy, only the opening prayer reflects the main theme of the gospel reading that we call upon the Father in faith at the eucharist, the way Peter and the apostles called upon Jesus in the gospel.

Sunday Preface V, about the command of the Father over all his creation, reflects the theme of the Old Testament and gospel reading where nature obeys his commands.

Of the prayers over the people, number 5, about remaining faithful to the Lord, number 9, about believing in Christ, and number 24, about persevering in the faith, all correspond to the theme of the Scriptures about proclaiming our faith and trust in the Lord to save us.

Sunday Preface I, about the characteristics of the Chosen People of God, and IV, about the history of salvation, reflect the theme of the reading from Romans about being called to the community of faith.

Number 6 of the prayers over the people adapts the theological problem of the relationship of Jew and Christian in faith to the experience of the present community where each of us needs a change of heart to follow our faith with greater integrity and fidelity.

Guidelines for the celebrant's introduction and comments:

INTRODUCTION

My brothers and sisters, we gather here this day because of our common faith and trust in the Father through his Son, Jesus Christ. And yet we also come because our faith and trust in him needs to be deepened and increased. May the celebration of the eucharist this day strengthen us in faith and in love as the pilgrim Church on earth.

PENITENTIAL RITE

You came to call all men to yourself: Lord, have mercy . . .

You taught the apostles to continue your work on earth: Christ, have mercy . . .

You strengthen the weak in their profession of faith: Lord, have mercy . . .

BEFORE THE READINGS

In the emphasis of an older theology one either possessed or did not possess "the faith." In recent theology the emphasis is rather on the quality and depth of our commitment. In today's readings the point at issue is that we move from "little faith" to more complete trust by the grace and power of God.

BEFORE THE EUCHARISTIC PRAYER

As we come to share this meal of our sanctification, let us pray for one another that the Lord will strengthen the faith of each of us and that together we may be a sign of true faith and love of Christ.

TWENTIETH SUNDAY IN ORDINARY TIME

When read by itself the point of the incident of Jesus and the Canaanite woman in the gospel of this Sunday is that while Jesus did not himself seek out the Gentiles, he still acknowledged her faith in him.

The setting of the story is still Jewish territory and the woman comes to him on her own. Clear indications that this is an exception are found in the necessary persistence of the woman in response to the indifference of Jesus, and the very harsh saying of verse 26 about food to humans (Israel) and throwing it to dogs (Gentiles). The woman is ultimately extolled for her great faith, and yet the price she has to pay for the curing of her daughter is this harsh dialogue with Jesus.

What happens in the liturgy of this Sunday, however, is that the Old Testament reading and the responsorial psalm lessen the severity of the Matthean Gospel by placing emphasis on the universality of redemption. This section of third Isaiah is the beginning of a return in this book to the universal scope of redemption envisioned in the early chapters ascribed to Isaiah himself. Here the Temple is not a place of exclusion or exclusiveness, but is the place where foreigners are welcomed, not merely tolerated. The holocausts and sacrifices are for *all* peoples who come to worship at the Temple, the house of prayer. Such a universalist perspective is not limited to Jewish sacrifices and liturgy, for from the earliest Christian celebrations, the eucharist always had a "catholic" and "apostolic" orientation. In the Didache, the prayer (of the eucharist or grace over meals) is that "as grain, once scattered on the hillsides, was in this broken bread made one, so from all lands thy church be gathered into thy kingdom by thy Son." The celebration of the eucharist is for the local community and "for all men so that sins may be forgiven."

The Epistle to the Romans provides another approach to the Jewish-Christian order and priority of evangelization. Paul admits clearly that in the Christian Church is the fulfillment of all the hopes and promises made to Israel, yet this fulfillment of Judaism is composed of Gentiles as well as Israelites. Paul here calls himself the apostle to the Gentiles (compare the statement of Jesus "to the lost sheep of the house of Israel") but still prays that the

Israelite rejection of Jesus may one day be reversed. Curiously, the lesson for the Church at Rome was to keep the community open to the Israelites, while Jesus allows Gentiles into a predominately Jewish congregation.

Both scriptural themes converge on the need for universality in Christian congregations. This is reflected in the alternative opening prayer which speaks of the love and care of the Father reaching beyond the boundaries of nation and race, because the boundaries set up by men should find no place in the hearts and experience of true Christians.

The proclamation of Sunday Preface VIII, about the characteristics of the Church as the body of Christ and the dwelling place of the Spirit, coincides with both scriptural themes. An alternative to this would be the proclamation of the fourth eucharistic prayer with its own preface since the prayer just before the Great Amen is for "all your people, and all who seek you with a sincere heart . . . and all the dead whose faith is known to you alone."

For the blessing at the conclusion of the eucharist, number 20 of the prayers over the people asks specifically that Christians may not be secure in isolation but may be filled with love for all men.

Guidelines for the celebrant's introduction and comments:

INTRODUCTION

My friends in Christ, we know that two of the marks of the church is that it is "catholic" and "apostolic." Similarly, our celebrations of the eucharist are also catholic and apostolic since we pray for all men and seek their response in faith to God's love for them. As we begin our celebration of these sacred mysteries, let us pray for the grace to be truly catholic and apostolic in our lives as well as in our prayers.

PENITENTIAL RITE

You came to call all men to the Father: Lord, have mercy . . .

Sundays in Ordinary Time

You loved all peoples, despite their race or origin: Christ, have mercy . . .

You sent the apostles to make disciples of all nations: Lord, have mercy . . .

BEFORE THE READING

In the three readings proclaimed for us today, the clear message is that the Christian faith knows no boundary because of race or creed. What should join us together is the realization of our common faith and the concern we have for those who do not believe as we do, not the barriers of our society of race, creed, and color.

BEFORE THE EUCHARISTIC PRAYER

The blood of Christ was shed for all men for the forgiveness of sins. May our prayer be not for ourselves, or even the needs of this community. May we pray that all men may become one body, one spirit in Christ.

TWENTY-FIRST SUNDAY IN ORDINARY TIME

The introduction to the gospel proclamation of the confession of Peter is from the book of Isaiah and speaks of the royalty and investiture of Eliakim. The reason Eliakim acceded to this position of authority and responsibility is that Shebna was plotting against Assyria with the help of the Egyptians in direct opposition to Isaiah's position of neutrality. The new leader receives all the homage due him, most especially the key of the House of David and the authority to open and close the door to the presence of a king, and so to grant or deny admission of a person to the king. Eliakim receives prestige and honor, but the inclusion of the statement about the misuse of this position by Shebna indicates that this authority grants rights and privileges only to those who exercise it faithfully.

The same is true of the authority of Peter in the classic text Matthew 16:16-18. These statements are not to be taken out of the context of Peter's confession of faith which precedes his selection and honor. Jesus changes his name from Simon Peter to "Rock" the way the Father changed Abram to Abraham and Saul was changed to Paul. Peter becomes the cornerstone of the early community and exercises authority not on his own, but for the sake of the integrity of the faith and the unity of the church. The authority of binding and loosing is to be exercised so that the community remains faithful to the revelation Jesus has taught them. It is to be exercised with the other members of the Church, for Jesus uses these same words when he addresses the disciples in 18:18, the gospel of the twenty-second Sunday in ordinary time.

In the climax to the story, Jesus gives them strict orders not to tell anyone about the fact that he is the Messiah, the Son of the living God since he was equally the Anointed One who would have to suffer before entering into his glory. As the disciples would have to remain faithful to the revelation Jesus made to them when they were given the power of binding and loosing, they would also have to exercise fidelity when preaching that as Messiah he had both to suffer and die before entering into his glory. The exercise of authority puts one in a precarious position; it requires fidelity, integrity and a commitment to serve the Lord, not oneself.

The second scriptural theme of the liturgy of the word is from the conclusion of Romans 11 where Paul offers praise and thanks to God for including everyone in the salvation he offered, first to Jews, then to the Gentiles. While the passage does not specifically refer to his argument of chapters nine through eleven, it does conclude the doctrinal portion of the Epistle with a prayer in praise of the wisdom of God. The preacher could speak on the theme of orthodoxy as meaning right worship as much as right theology and the task of learning about God.

The prayers of the liturgy do not reflect specifically either of the scriptural themes of the liturgy of the word, yet the opening prayer does speak of God's truth and hearing the word of God, both of which are essential for the proper exercise of authority in the present Church.

The prayer over the gifts asks that the people may receive the peace and unity of the kingdom even now as they share in the eucharist.

The theme of the confession of faith as that which binds the Church together is reflected in Sunday Preface VIII, whereas the theme of the love of God for man through Jesus is found in Sunday Preface II.

Of the prayers over the people, number 5 asks that the people who celebrate the eucharist may remain faithful to the Lord, and number 20 asks that the God who has already granted us his mercy may continue to show his love for the Church and help us share that love for all men.

Guidelines for the celebrant's introduction and comments:

INTRODUCTION

My brothers and sisters, in today's gospel the apostle Peter makes a profession of faith in Christ as the Messiah sent from God. We gather here this day to make that same profession in our worship and in the quality of our lives this coming week. May we pause now as we begin our celebration to pray that our response to God's love to us might be a faith that is living and honest.

PENITENTIAL RITE

You are the Anointed one of the Father: Lord, have mercy . . .

You are the Messiah sent from God: Christ, have mercy . . .

You are our Savior and our Lord: Lord, have mercy . . .

BEFORE THE READINGS

To assume a role of leadership in the Church is to accept the responsibility of growing in the faith and fostering that growth in others. Today's readings present for our reflection an example of both a proper and an improper use of authority.

BEFORE THE EUCHARISTIC PRAYER

The profession of faith which Peter made in Christ is the same profession we make during this eucharistic prayer. May we continue to make this act of faith by the quality of the lives we lead when we are sent forth when this celebration is completed.

TWENTY-SECOND SUNDAY IN ORDINARY TIME

The context of the gospel for this Sunday is the revelation Jesus offers to his disciples apart from the declarations of the Sermon on the Mount for the crowds. In the beginning of today's gospel Jesus gets to the heart of the matter for he begins by indicating that he must suffer and be put to death before being raised up on the third day. He does not indicate the precise methods of the suffering and the cause of death, for his purpose here is to present the pattern of his own life as the model for the believers who follow him. The disciples are to endure suffering and trial for their faith in Christ and are to take up their cross in imitation of the suffering of their Lord. The point at issue is defining what helps a person's faith and what binds that profession. The conclusion of the pericope is a typical Matthean addition for he indicates that the return of the Son of Man in glory will mean the beginning of the judgment of the "faithful." One's conduct and priorities are to be judged before disciples will be called to share in the glory of the kingdom. The figure of Peter and his question to Jesus is in a curious place in the gospel for his opposition to this saying of Jesus follows his clear confession of faith and his selection as a figure of authority and influence. Yet, the figure of

Peter is easily the model of all believers for it is easier to accept the Messiahship of Jesus when it means glory and eternal life than when it involves denial, renunciation, and suffering.

The second theme of the liturgy of the word is taken from the beginning of Paul's exhortation in Romans 12. It is characteristic of the writer to turn from theology and doctrinal explanations to instructive exhortation, and in the Epistle to the Romans, the exhortation is the basis of chapters 12 and 13. The theological introduction to this section (verses 1-2) asks that, like the cultic sacrifices of the old law, the community offer themselves as sacrifices, not by their death but by living according to God's will rather than abiding by what is the common experience of this age. The rest of this chapter presents general ethical instruction and, unlike the letters to the Corinthians, is not based on any particular scandal or problem experienced in the Roman church.

The prayers of the liturgy do not reflect the main scriptural theme of the day, but the alternate opening prayer does reflect the second reading from Romans where we pray that God's will may be done by the community and what he values may become the values which the Christian community will live by.

Of the Sunday prefaces, number I speaks of the humility of the Son of God, number II speaks of the suffering and death of Jesus, number IV refers to the suffering of Jesus, and number VIII refers to the blood of the sacrifice of the Lord, hence the theme of the first passion prediction in Matthew's Gospel finds ample expression in these prayers.

The best expression of this theme for the blessing is number 17 of the prayers over the people which indicates the love of God through the agony of Christ on the cross.

The theme of the exhortation in Romans 12 is only indirectly reflected in the reference to the characteristics of the pilgrim Church in Sunday Preface I, where they now proclaim the mighty works of God, and the exhortation that the community live according to the will of God is found in the prayers over the people number 4, about living a holy life; number 9 is sharing the gift of God's love with each other, number 11 is readiness to do the Lord's will, and number 21 is avoiding whatever is evil.

Guidelines for the celebrant's introduction and comments:

INTRODUCTION

My brothers and sisters, we join in our common worship this Sunday to praise and thank the Father for the redemption he accomplished through the suffering and death of his Son. May we who share this banquet of salvation also be willing to share the humiliation and suffering of Jesus, our Savior.

PENITENTIAL RITE

You humbled youself to become one like us: Lord, have mercy . . .

You endured suffering and death for our salvation: Christ, have mercy . . .

You rose on the third day to share your Father's glory: Lord, have mercy . . .

BEFORE THE READINGS

Renunciation and self-discipline for the sake of the Gospel is the key to understanding today's Scripture readings. To share in the glory of the Father requires that we first share in the passion and death by renunciation and suffering for his sake in our lives.

BEFORE THE EUCHARISTIC PRAYER

As we come to share the banquet of our redemption and salvation, may we receive the grace and strength from this eucharist to humble ourselves to share the sufferings which profession of the Christian faith requires.

TWENTY-THIRD SUNDAY IN ORDINARY TIME

The vocation of a prophet, as envisioned in terms of Ezekiel's oracles, is to judge the evil and the wicked and to dissuade them from their ways. The prophet has the responsibility of announcing the judgment of God, not his own judgment, and nonfulfillment of preaching the message of God involves death for the prophet, whereas he will save his life if he is faithful to the message given him to preach. The theme of judgment in the form of fraternal correction is the focus of attention in the gospel of Matthew where the verses proclaimed this Sunday follow the section on the lost sheep in 18:10-14. Fraternal correction is one way in which the followers of Jesus continue his ministry by seeking and finding those that are lost. Matthew makes it explicit that the extension of mercy and forgiveness is not limited to apologizing for what one has done; rather the situation involves anyone who has wronged us and deserves our forgiveness. The stages of this forgiveness are first private between the two parties, before some others to authenticate the action, or ultimately before the local community of faith. The power of binding and loosing which was already given to the early community in Matthew 16:16-18, is now to be shared explicitly by all the members of the assembly. In this connection, the authority is given to judge, to condemn, and to forgive a member of the Church for a specific deed, rather than to decide doctrinal matters. The promise of the presence of the Lord in worship assemblies is a concrete expression of his pledge to remain with the community until the end of the world (Matthew 28:20).

Significantly, the link between the Old Testament and the gospel selections is the classic psalm used at morning prayer, asking to come into the presence of the Lord and to sing his praises.

The second theme for the liturgy of the word is that of Romans 13 about love as the summary of the whole law of Christ. It may be regretted that this is the only part of the moral exhortation of Romans 12-13 which is proclaimed at the Sunday liturgy, yet this passage includes the whole of the law in a condensed form: "love is the fulfillment of the law."

The prayers of the liturgy do not directly reflect the main scriptural theme for this Sunday, but the alternative form of the opening prayer does express the teaching of Paul in the second reading—in God alone are perfect justice, mercy and love, and the follower of Jesus is to share these with the rest of the community. Sunday Preface VIII is the most accurate description of the Church, which is called in the Scriptures to fraternal correction and prayer, for in this preface the love of God and the sacrifice of Jesus are the basis of the love that is shared in the body of Christ and the dwelling place of the Spirit.

Of the prayers over the people, number 2, about the love of believers for each other, number 5, about rejoicing in God's mercy, and number 23, about remaining close to the Lord and to each other in prayer, are the blessings which carry out the main theme of the Scriptures.

Of the Sunday prefaces which give praise for the love of God for us, II, about his humiliation, and VII, about the great love of Jesus as our redeemer, form the basis and model for the love for each other urged by Paul in the second reading.

Of the prayers over the people, number 2, about perfect love for each other is the best expression in a blessing for the theme of the reading from Romans.

Guidelines for the celebrant's introduction and comments:

INTRODUCTION

My brothers and sisters, the Scripture readings proclaim that honesty and integrity should mark our relationship with each other. We come to this celebration of Christ's love to pray that we in turn will offer to others that same love and concern. We come to the presence of the Lord this day for his healing and sanctification.

PENITENTIAL RITE

You came to bring us the Father's love: Lord, have mercy . . .

You call us this day to show your mercy to others: Christ, have mercy . . .

You are present where two or three are gathered in your name: Lord, have mercy . . .

BEFORE THE READINGS

The golden rule that we do to others what we would have them do to us is changed in today's readings since the demand of Jesus is not to act according to strict justice but to extend his mercy whenever and wherever it is needed.

BEFORE THE EUCHARISTIC PRAYER

We come to this table to receive the Lord's body and blood so that we may live according to his unity, love, and peace. As we approach to receive this eucharist, may we receive the strength and humility we need to extend God's mercy to others.

TWENTY-FOURTH SUNDAY IN ORDINARY TIME

The introduction to the Matthean instruction on mutual forgiveness is taken from the Old Testament reading from Sirach which speaks of forgiving others so that "when you pray, your own sins will be forgiven." What differentiates this from the teaching of Jesus on forgiveness is that here the motivation tends to be self-justifying. To experience forgiveness from God, one must make sure his own accounts are in order. The misunderstanding here is that this scale of measuring justice according to "an eye for an eye and a tooth for a tooth" has come to an end in the freely given mercy and love of the Christ. The Christian can no longer forgive so as to receive an equal portion in return.

The psalm response more accurately reflects the New Testament teaching, for it proclaims the Lord as kind and merciful "slow to anger, rich in compassion," for his kindness and mercy do not depend on man's *initiative* of forgiving others, but it does require that man *respond* to God's forgiveness in showing that same mercy to others.

In the beginning of the gospel Jesus responds to Peter's question by multiplying a symbolic number by another symbolic number to reach an infinite quantity in reply—the point being that the number of times forgiveness should be offered cannot be measured. Furthermore, the royal official needed a great deal of understanding and forgiveness because his debt was quite large; his response in not forgiving the debt of another over a lesser sum is precisely the kind of forgiveness the Lord did not come to bring. The original stage of the parable from Jesus' teaching ends here —man responds to God's mercy by extending that mercy to others. What has happened in the elaboration of the story, however, is that allegorical details have colored the purpose and import of the teaching of Jesus. He will forever be merciful to us, and our forgiving others is not a condition for his generosity toward us; God is faithful to man even though man is unfaithful to God. Man's business instincts and rabbinic casuistry have no place in the face of this parable. God's ways are indeed not man's ways for his mercy endures forever.

The second theme presented in the liturgy of the word comes from Romans 14 where the context of Paul's instruction is differences among various members of the Church over their obligations and responsibilities in the practice of the faith. We live and die responsible to God alone. The unity of the Church is not based on uniformity of practices and customs, but is a unity in the essentials of the faith. The concern is whether or not our central beliefs are the same; the manifestation of those beliefs and how individuals or certain communities live their faith is not a matter of concern for Paul. There is to be a plurality in the religious practice of those who share one faith in the one Lord of all.

The opening prayer of the liturgy asks that we may experience the forgiveness of God in our lives, the way the official received mercy from his king and master.

The prayer after communion prays that the experience of the eucharist will influence our actions so that others may receive the love of God from us which we receive at the sharing of the Lord's body and blood.

Sunday Preface III speaks of the infinite power of God's loving plan of salvation and may be understood to include his mercy and forgiveness.

Of the prayers over the people, number 2 speaks of the protection and grace the Lord bestows on his people by the eucharist, number 5 asks that the community always rejoice in the Lord's mercy, number 8 speaks of the Father's generosity and love, and number 23 asks that the community be strengthened by God's grace, and remain close to him in prayer and concern for one another.

The prayer over the gifts more accurately reiterates the second scriptural theme since it acknowledges the worship of each one present and asks that salvation come to all of them.

Sunday Preface VIII speaks of the unity of the Church as a unity of faith in the Trinity and then cites the Church as the Body of Christ, with expansive biblical image by which the Church in its many members and functions is still considered one.

Of the prayers over the people, number 23 speaks of the unity of the Church based on fraternal love and prayer.

Guidelines for the celebrant's introduction and comments:

INTRODUCTION

My brothers and sisters, we gather together to proclaim the kindness and mercy of our Savior and Lord. May we who are strengthened by this sacred rite seek to extend to others that same mercy and love. May we pause in silence now to realize the power and love of Christ in our midst.

PENITENTIAL RITE

You forgive us our sins, and do not judge us for them: Lord, have mercy . . .

You are slow to anger and rich in compassion: Christ, have mercy . . .

You do not deal with us according to our misdeeds: Lord, have mercy . . .

BEFORE THE READINGS

Giving so that we receive in return may be a common practice, but it has no biblical base. The revelation of God's word reminds us that his forgiveness is freely granted to those most in need of his love. God does not barter for our thanks, he invites us to the eucharist to share his love again.

BEFORE THE EUCHARISTIC PRAYER

We gather around this altar to give the Lord our glory and praise for the gifts of this eucharist by which we share again in the body and blood which were shed for us "and for all men that sins may be forgiven."

TWENTY-FIFTH SUNDAY IN ORDINARY TIME

Recent literature on the usefulness of Scripture in our present age has indicated that much of the imagery of the Bible is foreign to our everyday experience. The agrarian imagery affects fewer and fewer people, and talk of kingdom and the king of a country does not rest comfortably with those for whom democracy is a way of life. But it must be admitted that these are symptoms of the much more basic problem involved with understanding the Scriptures—our unwillingness to listen when the authors say what we would rather not hear, when the readings don't happen to agree with our already established life style. And while all of this may be true in general terms, it is most especially true in the readings for this Sunday. The Old Testament reading from Isaiah states quite clearly that God's ways are not ours and his thoughts are not always our own. The psalm sets up the gospel proclamation, for in it we pray that the Lord may be near to all who call upon him. The problem arises, however, in the gospel when the Lord shows his mercy to those who do not seem to deserve it! The laborers who worked all day expected more than those who worked just an hour. Even though they agreed on a wage, the fact that they worked more hours would almost require that they be given more. The strict economy of personnel management and the American way of life is slashed when this gospel is read, for strict calculation and reward are demolished in favor of a strong biblical lesson for all the members of the community; no one of us deserves the mercy of God, but when we receive it we should be most grateful. The problem arises when God shows it to "other" people. We become jealous when another receives God's favor—but are humbly grateful when we receive it ourselves.

The second scriptural theme for this Sunday is taken from the letter to the Philippians, chapter one, instead of the letter to the Romans which concluded last Sunday. Paul wrote to the Philippians while he was in prison and in the throes of torment. If the result be martyrdom or release, he maintains that his ministry will continue since by martyrdom many will hear of his mission, and by release, he will again be able to be actively engaged in preaching. The apostle comes to no decision but uses this opportunity to teach his audience the meaning of death; for Paul "life means Christ, hence dying is so much gain."

Both forms of the opening prayer of the liturgy speak of the justice of God at work through his mercy and love and hence point to the lesson of the gospel about his generosity. Sunday Preface II speaks of God's love for sinful man, and VII speaks of God's great love in sending us his Son as our redeemer. Of the prayers over the people, 8 speaks about the Lord's generosity and love, 5 speaks of the Lord blessing his people with his mercy, and 17 asks that the Lord look upon us with his love, the love which Jesus showed us by his passion and death.

The only vague reference to the dilemma Paul presents in the Philippian reading is found in the opening prayer of the liturgy about the eternal life prepared for all of us. The Sunday preface does, however, present the model of Christ's death as an example for the Christian in I, when his redemption has made us his chosen people, IV, where suffering leads to rising to everlasting life, and VI, where the gifts of the Spirit who raised Jesus from the dead is a foreshadow of our own Paschal feast in heaven.

No one of the prayers over the people is more adequate than the others in carrying through the theme of the Philippian reading.

Guidelines for the celebrant's introduction and comments:

INTRODUCTION

My brothers and sisters, we come together to celebrate our common faith and trust in the mercy and love of God. Today's first reading reminds us that our ways are not those of the Lord and that we must submit ourselves to his judgment. May we realize the power of the word of God which calls us to a life of conversion to the ways of the Lord.

PENITENTIAL RITE

You came to preach the good news to all men: Lord, have mercy . . .

You came to release captives and give sight to the blind: Christ, have mercy . . .

You came to give freely of your Father's generous love: Lord, have mercy . . .

BEFORE THE READINGS

The conventional criteria for wages paid for services rendered is upset by the gospel of this day which speaks in terms of God's generosity to all men despite their performance. How willing are we to live according to the teaching that "the last shall be first and the first shall be last."

BEFORE THE EUCHARISTIC PRAYER

As we draw near to this table of God's mercy and love let us lay aside our standards of judgment and join in thanking the Father for the gift of redemption through his Son, our Savior and Lord.

TWENTY-SIXTH SUNDAY IN ORDINARY TIME

The selection of the Old Testament lesson from Ezekiel is an appropriate introduction to the gospel proclamation for this Sunday. The point at issue in the first reading is the determination of the individual believer to turn away from his past sins and live according to what is right and just. The two opposites presented for the person's choice involve iniquity and wickedness on the one hand, and virtue and what is right and just on the other. The decision rests at the level of action, not mere verbal agreement. This sets up the gospel reading where verbal affirmations come and go, but the man of integrity performs the act of virtue and lives according to what is right.

The folksy parable of a father and his two sons and the work to be done in their vineyard soon gives way to the statement of Jesus that tax collectors and prostitutes gain entrance into the kingdom before those who say the right thing but perform what is wrong.

A person's past does not necessarily determine his future life. What is important is the moment of conversion and true allegiance in the present and the future. Repentance and conversion are continual commands for the believer and should not be restricted to a special time or season like Lent. The process of conversion requires many adjustments and changes if the believer is to fully realize the demand to live according to God's wisdom, not man's.

The second theme of the Scripture readings is from the second chapter of the letter to the Philippians. The short form of the reading indicates that the emphasis in preaching should be on the exhortation which precedes the Christ-hymn of the longer version. The key to the reading and the morality of this section of Philippians is that we are to model ourselves after Christ's act of self-emptying as he took on our human condition. We also must humble ourselves if we are to live in complete unanimity of love, without rivalry or conceit, never allowing ourselves to have a superior attitude toward others for we are to look to others' interests rather than to our own. Both scriptural themes require self-examination and conversion from a former way of life, and in both instances, we pray for the mercy of God to help us begin again with his help and guidance.

Both forms of the opening prayer speak of God's unbounded mercy and forgiveness and set the proper context for both themes of the liturgy of the word. Sunday Preface VII speaks of the great love of God who sent his Son as our redeemer, while III more accurately reflects the theme of the Philippians exhortation since it describes the power of God to rescue and save us through the salvation of the God-Man, Jesus.

Of the prayers over the people, number 1 speaks of the mercy of God on his people which sets the context for any conversion on our part; number 6 tells of the Lord's concern for his people even when they stray; number 15 asks for God's mercy to help the faithful avoid what displeases the Father, and number 17 asks that the love of the Father which caused Christ to suffer for our salvation may continue to be with us in our need.

Guidelines for the celebrant's introduction and comments:

INTRODUCTION

My friends in Christ, we gather this day to turn away from our everyday concerns and turn toward the Lord and Savior of us all. May we conform ourselves to his word and trust always in his mercy and love for us.

PENITENTIAL RITE

You humbled yourself to be born of the Virgin: Lord, have mercy . . .

You took the form of a slave to be born in the likeness of men: Christ, have mercy . . .

You are forever our Lord and Savior: Lord, have mercy . . .

BEFORE THE READINGS

It is a virtue in our society to take a person at his word. The readings of this liturgy, however, place the priority not on words but on the actions a person performs. The test of the faithful man is whether he follows through on his promises.

BEFORE THE EUCHARISTIC PRAYER

We are brought face to face with the author and cause of our salvation in the presence of the Lord at the eucharist. May we live as men and women who are transformed by this sacrament and whose actions reflect the words we now speak.

TWENTY-SEVENTH SUNDAY IN ORDINARY TIME

One of the principles of the exegesis and interpretation of the synoptic Gospels is to compare the account found in one with its counterpart in the other Gospels. This procedure is especially helpful in interpreting the parable in today's gospel for the original form of the parable as Jesus proposed it is found in traces from Luke and the later writing e.g., the apocryphal Gospel of Thomas.

The original form of the parable emphasized the industry of the tenant farmers as they stopped at nothing, even to the point of killing invaders, to keep hold of the vineyard. The intensity of the concern of the vinedressers in pursuing their task is the model for the concern of the followers of Jesus to pursue and preserve the kingdom of God. The more allegorical interpretation in Matthew's Gospel changes the emphasis to the rejection by the house of Israel of the prophets and the Messiah. Hence, to facilitate the understanding of the Jewish-Christian community, Matthew gives special emphasis to the son of the owner of the field and describes him by using Psalm 118 about the Father's rejected son becoming the cornerstone of the new Israel. In allegorizing the parable the primitive community relied on the song of Isaiah 5 to complete some of its details, and it is for this reason that this song is chosen for this Sunday's first reading. That the Lectionary editors want to emphasize the allegorical interpretation of the parable is obvious in the responsorial psalm in which the vineyard of the Lord is identified with the house of Israel. The rejection of the Messiah can take on many forms and limiting it to the Jewish rejection of Jesus is to miss the reason why it is read for the Christian community, when the vineyard of the Lord is the present assembly of God's people.

The second theme of the liturgy of the word is taken from the letter to the Philippians in which Paul speaks of the peace of Christ reigning in the heart of believers, and offering to the Lord every form of prayer as well as the quality of the lives we lead. The necessity of prayer for the full realization of the Christian vocation may be a profitable theme to explore especially at the liturgical prayer of the Christian people, the Sunday eucharist.

The alternate form of the opening prayer of the liturgy is a fitting introduction to the Old Testament and gospel readings since it speaks about having the courage to stand before God's truth, which revealed in these readings necessarily causes pain for those who reject the Son of God in any way.

The reality of salvation despite man's rejection is the theme of Sunday Preface III, and the disobedience and rejection of man are restored by the obedience of Jesus in Preface VII; either of these prefaces may be proclaimed to coincide with the liturgy of the word. Another choice would be to proclaim the fourth eucharistic prayer with its own preface because of its emphasis on the rejection of God by man and the proclamation of the Gospel to those who would accept: the poor, the imprisoned, and those in sorrow.

Of the prayers over the people, number 2, about remaining faithful to the Lord, number 5, about fidelity and God's mercy, and number 6, about straying from belief and needing God's mercy for conversion, are all proper selections for this Sunday.

The opening prayer of the liturgy speaks of the peace of Christ and the way of his salvation and reflects the appeal of Paul in the second reading to dismiss our anxieties and let Christ's peace reign in our hearts.

Sunday Preface V reflects the Philippian reading for it speaks of man's vocation to return praise to the Father through the Son for the gift of the eucharist.

Of the prayers over the people number 4, about being made holy and avoiding evil reflects the moral instruction of the second reading, and number 11 speaks of the blessing of God we receive at the eucharist to enable us to do his will.

Guidelines for the celebrant's introduction and comments:

INTRODUCTION

My brothers and sisters, we gather for this act of prayer and praise to the Father for the gift of our common faith in him through his Son. May we who speak this faith never fail to live our faith and always remain true to the ways of the Son of God.

PENITENTIAL RITE

Lord Jesus, you have revealed to us the Father's will: Lord, have mercy . . .

Lord Jesus, you have reconciled us with your heavenly Father: Christ, have mercy . . .

Lord Jesus, you are the Son of the Most High: Lord, have mercy . . .

BEFORE THE READINGS

At first glance, the readings we hear this day appear to be addressed to those of the house of Israel who refused to believe in Jesus. Yet they are also addressed to us because we Christians are also guilty of worshipping other gods of power and pride and thereby of dabbling in the sin of rejecting him as the Son of God.

BEFORE THE EUCHARISTIC PRAYER

As we offer our prayer of praise and thanksgiving to the Father through his Son, we pray for ourselves that the peace of Christ may reign in our hearts and that we may remain faithful to the Father by the grace of his Son and our Savior.

TWENTY-EIGHTH SUNDAY IN ORDINARY TIME

The imagery of the Lord providing a majestic banquet for his people and caring for their every need does not find its origin in the book of Isaiah, but it does give a significant poetic and dramatic force to the first reading of today's liturgy. Among the images of God in the Old Testament few are as compelling as that of the provider of a banquet of refreshment, the Lord who will extinguish death forever, the kind of God who is so concerned as to wipe away tears from those who mourn, who always remains with his people to shepherd them. And yet this is the very description of God found in the Old Testament reading and the responsorial psalm. Despite this familiarity with God and the intimacy with him at the banquet of salvation, other images of God in the book of Isaiah speak of him as totally other. In the parable of St. Matthew's gospel, the invitation is extended to the many, but demands are definitely made on those who accept and respond. The sharing in the messianic banquet of the eucharist as a foretaste of the eschatological banquet in the kingdom of the Father also requires that certain conditions be met and that we live according to his ways. This is one of the possible interpretations of the man without a wedding garment.

The proper understanding of the meaning of the eucharist runs a course between the caricatured extremes of "free and easy access" to the table of the Lord and the reception of the eucharist as "a reward for doing good." To be baptized and a member of the body of Christ requires of us a way of life that is in conformity with the Gospel we believe in. Sharing in the eucharist and responding to the invitation to participate in it strengthens those who seek to live according to the will of God and sanctifies those who know their need of God.

The second theme of the liturgy of the word is taken from an expression of gratitude on Paul's part for the charity of the Philippians, as he closes his letter to them. But this courtesy in thanking them is not without its theme and theological reason for at the same time he speaks of detachment from an abundance of this life and reliance on the riches of God's grace to fill all our wants and desires.

The alternative form of the opening prayer speaks of an image of

God who forever cares for his people and also reflects the theme of the Old Testament reading and the responsorial psalm.

Both the prayer over the gifts and the prayer after communion coincide with the theme of the banquet set by the Father for his people since they speak of the sharing in the eucharist of God's glory even here on earth.

The Father's plan of salvation and the redemption through Christ form the core of Sunday Preface III, and the love of God the Father by sending the Son and the Spirit in Preface VI are both appropriate selections to carry through the theme of the image of God and the banquet of salvation of the day's readings.

Many of the prayers over the people speak of the love of the Father and the banquet of salvation but number 18 is particularly appropriate because it emphasizes the renewal of the eucharist and our constant need for rebirth by God's mercy.

Part of the alternative form of the opening prayer also coincides with the second reading for it speaks of the loving kindness of the Father so that in practicing the detachment Paul speaks of we need only rely on his love and care for us. That the Lord supplies all our needs fully is part of the message of Paul to the Philippians and is part of the prayer of praise we offer in Sunday Prefaces III and V.

Of the prayers over the people, number 19 reflects the theme of the second reading for it speaks of being enriched by God's mercy and love, and that our response to that love is our prayer of praise, especially in the eucharist.

The following may be used as explanations and comments.

INTRODUCTION

My friends, we come before this throne of God's glory and this table of his grace and love so that we might become sharers in this banquet of our salvation. May we pause for a moment now to realize the presence of God in our midst and to make of our worship an honest expression of our faith and prayer.

PENITENTIAL RITE

You are the shepherd who continually cares for his people: Lord, have mercy . . .

You feed us this day with the food of heaven: Christ, have mercy . . .

You invite us to share in the banquet of salvation: Lord, have mercy . . .

BEFORE THE READINGS

To refuse an invitation is a matter of discourtesy. But to refuse the Lord's invitation to share the banquet of his love is an act of disbelief. As we learn of the image of God and his love for us in these readings, let us approach this eucharist eagerly and with heartfelt thanks.

BEFORE THE EUCHARISTIC PRAYER

We come to express our thanks and praise to the Father for this meal of fellowship and redemption. May we who share this banquet realize the majesty and splendor of the Father who feeds us as his chosen people.

TWENTY-NINTH SUNDAY IN ORDINARY TIME

The task of the Church in her teaching role is to apply the perennially valid word of God to the changing circumstances of men's lives. The question which needs to be answered repeatedly and the problem that continually needs to be solved is just what does a particular scriptural passage mean almost two thousand years after it was originally spoken or written down. And there is no more critical issue than that raised by today's gospel reading of the relationship between church and state. Rendering to God and rendering to Caesar is especially difficult in a society where civil disobedience is often offered as the answer. The heart of the gospel passage for our day is that each requires and demands rightful allegiance provided that the demands of the state do not require that one go against the demands of the community of the faith. Questions of conscience are always in the forefront of the consideration of the believer, either individually or collectively. Recent Church statements do not endorse a complete separation between the secular and the saved, the things of men and the things of God, the social and the religious. The very title of the Pastoral Constitution on the Church in the Modern World and the encyclicals of Pope John, *Pacem In Terris*, and of Pope Paul in *Populorum Progressio* indicate that the Church must be involved in the affairs of men for men need clarification to be derived from the insights into the word of God. The biblical notion of the community of faith as leaven for the rest of society, and the believers in the Word as a sign to the rest of the world of God's ways are very much to the forefront of recent Church teaching and emphasis. To be concerned with the things of God does not mean that the concerns of men are any less important.

The responsorial psalm gives the believer's perspective to all of this, in that we give honor and glory to the Lord alone, not to a state at the same time. However, the Christian's duty includes participation in promoting the common good of society.

The second scriptural theme for the day is from the opening of the First Epistle to the Thessalonians. This is the earliest of Paul's writings and in it he compliments the community on the way they have proven their faith in being considerate in their love for each other, and of their constant hope in the Lord.

The introduction to the opening prayer and the text of the prayer itself clearly reflects the gospel of the day in praying for Christian service toward God and man, a theme which is also part of the prayer over the gifts.

Sunday Preface V, about man as the steward of creation, is the only one that reflects in any way the theme of the gospel. A far better solution is to use the fourth eucharistic prayer and preface which emphasize those who share the Christian faith but who must still live in and be a part of the world, that they may live no longer for themselves but for the Lord and the spread of his Gospel.

Of the prayers over the people, number 7, about the devotion of the Christians to doing good, number 11, about doing God's will in this world, and number 15, about granting the faithful true judgment that they avoid whatever hinders their Christian faith, are all appropriate selections to reflect the main scriptural theme.

None of the prayers of the liturgy of the day reflect the theme of the reading from first Thessalonians, but Sunday Preface I, about the Church being called out of darkness by the power of God, and VIII, about the community united to the Trinity, do coincide with the positive picture of the Church presented in this reading.

The example of the Thessalonian community in their love for each other can be the model of love for the assembly that is sanctified by the eucharist. This theme is found in numbers 2, 9, and 23 of the prayers over the people.

Guidelines for the celebrant's introduction and comments:

INTRODUCTION

My friends, we are gathered this day to offer our prayer of praise and homage to the Father for his grace to us as well as to pray for the needs of all mankind. May we be faithful in this coming week to the demands of today's gospel to render our service to God and our fellow man.

PENITENTIAL RITE

Lord Jesus, you call us to lives of willing service: Lord, have mercy . . .

Lord Jesus, to you belongs all glory and honor: Christ, have mercy . . .

Lord Jesus, in your word is our truth: Lord, have mercy . . .

BEFORE THE READINGS

In a world which discusses conscientious objection as often as it does military service, and civil disobedience as well as civil service, the proclamation of the word of God calls each of us to critical reflection on the meaning of living our Christian faith in the modern world in which we live.

BEFORE THE EUCHARISTIC PRAYER

As we come to this table of God's grace and glory, may this sacrament enable us to live our faith according to the demands of the Gospel and to put Gospel values before the things of this world.

THIRTIETH SUNDAY IN ORDINARY TIME

The context for the Gospel teaching about the greatest commandment of the Law is the questioning of the Pharisees about tributes to Caesar, the questioning of the Sadducees about the resurrection, and finally the questioning of both the Pharises and Sadducees through the lawyer about priorities of the Law of God. The response of Jesus to each of these difficult questions is to respond to them with surprising answers, and yet the most traditional of these is in the gospel read today. For Jesus took two parts of the Old Testament law about love of God and neighbor, and made these a new teaching by joining them together and calling them the basis for the whole law. The concept of these commandments of love being the basis for the Christian life is the thesis of the First Letter of John where he declares quite openly that to live in the light of Christ means unequivocally that we are to love our neighbor and if we do not, we remain in darkness (John 2:7-11). Jesus gives no new commandment at all, but informs his questioners that these are the basis of his law.

One interesting aspect of this saying of Jesus is that love of self and love of neighbor are part of our love of God. Instead of playing down self-love and cautioning his audience about pride, Jesus maintains that self-love, in the form of self-acceptance, and self-knowledge, can be the most painful of all acts of love and yet love for others only becomes authentic when a person truly struggles to love, accept and know himself. The dimension of social responsibility in the act of loving God comes next for we love God precisely in the act and determination to love others. This manifestation of our true love for God is the trying, yet necessary, act of love for others.

The second scriptural theme continues the reading from first Thessalonians and in it Paul compliments this community on their adherence to faith in the one God as opposed to their former belief in idols. The current application of this reading could be the questioning of present day communities as to their many gods in this world, and their allegiance to the one true God. To serve God means to serve him alone and not to be lost in the distraction of false gods.

The opening prayer of the liturgy asks that this community grow in love and do what the love of God requires in their lives, and so coincides with the theme of the gospel of the day. Also, the prayer over the gifts and the prayer after communion speak of rendering glory to the Father by our service to each other and that the sharing of the eucharist have its effect in the lives of the community. Sunday Preface VII speaks of God's love for us through Jesus, and the eucharist is our continual sharing in that love. The expression of our love for God in love for other men is the basis of numbers 2, 9, and 23 of the prayers over the people.

The alternative form of the opening prayer corresponds with Paul's message to the Thessalonians since he complimented their perseverance in faith in the one God, and the prayer states that nothing good can come unless it comes from the covenant between God and man through Jesus' sacrifice.

One of the themes of the Thessalonian reading is man's imitation of the Lord and this finds adequate expression in Sunday Preface III.

The blessing should be taken from number 5 of the prayers over the people, about remaining faithful to the profession of the faith, or number 24, about preserving those who believe from anything that endangers that profession.

Guidelines for the celebrant's introduction and comments:

INTRODUCTION

My brothers and sisters in Christ, we come together to hear the word of the Lord this day and to be renewed by the celebration of this sacrament. The message of today's gospel is that we cannot live our Christianity in isolation from others, since love for God is defined in terms of love for one another. As we begin this celebration of God's love for us, may we in turn share that love with those most in need of God's mercy . . .

PENITENTIAL RITE

You have called us out of darkness to share in your divine light: Lord, have mercy . . .

You have called us to profess our faith in you alone: Christ, have mercy . . .

You invite us to share in this sacrament of your love: Lord, have mercy . . .

BEFORE THE READINGS

A key word in our society and in the business world is "priorities." We are constantly being called upon to establish priorities of a Christian: to love God by loving one another.

Sundays in Ordinary Time

BEFORE THE EUCHARISTIC PRAYER

We acclaim the love of God made present for us at this eucharist through his Son Jesus. May our prayer through him, with him, and in him, assist us in our lives of sharing that love with all men.

THIRTY-FIRST SUNDAY IN ORDINARY TIME

Chapter 23 of the Gospel of St. Matthew is a summary of the theologizing of Matthew about the situation of the community of his day. His approach seems quite harsh and very direct in its accusations and examples, but his concern for the Christian community has motivated the severity of this pronouncement.

There are two levels of interpretation for the selection of this Sunday's gospel—the level of the professionals in religion, and the level of the rest of the community. The problem with the professionals is essentially that they do not practice what they preach. And the result is heavy burdens for the community due to a hypocritical clergy. But the believers are not exonerated either since all that is said about the professional purveyors of organized religion is said of the community in the same gospel. A religious practice that is socially acceptable and status-granting is no Christianity. Hypocrisy does not affect the leaders alone, it affects all the followers as well. And the accusations did not end with first century Christianity, for the Church in our day experiences its measure of Sunday worshippers and weekday atheists, people who learn and study to "make the sacraments" but for whom the sacraments are nothing more than external rituals—an extrinsicist Christianity of the worst sort. The level that the gospel reaches is the level of personal and communal conversion, and one that needs the constant goading of this and similar gospel proclamations.

The first reading states that this is a people who had wandered from the way of belief in God, a theme which Matthew asserts in many ways in chapters 6-7, but which he states explicitly in 7:13-14. "Enter through the narrow gate. The gate that leads to damnation is wide, the road is clear, and many choose to travel it. But how narrow is the gate that leads to life, how rough the road, and how few are there who find it." The task of both preacher and the assembly gathered for worship is to open themselves to the severity of the sentence in the gospel and interpret it as referring to this place and to this generation. Although the cultural supports for Catholicism are fewer than in past generations, the true believer is one who chooses his faith without any such supports at all.

The second theme of the readings is Paul's complimentary introduction to the letter to the Thessalonians where he thanks them for the reception they gave to the word that he preached to them. It is not a word that one preaches easily or on his own terms, but it is one that needs the verbalization and application through the Church's minister. Paul is especially grateful, therefore, that they received the word as from God, not men. The preacher of the word of God is well aware of his responsibility in proclaiming and preaching that word for he asks in the prayer before the gospel that the Lord will cleanse his heart and lips as he did Isaiah's for he is aware that it is God's word that is to be preached, not his own, or on his own terms.

Both of the opening prayers of the liturgy this Sunday speak in terms of the gospel for they refer to living the faith and not merely listening to it. Sunday Preface V speaks of the whole community offering their praise to the Father, not merely of the Church's minister, and VIII refers to the theme of hypocrisy indirectly because it speaks of those who still must profess and live their faith, and who can do so only through the transforming power of the eucharist they celebrate.

Of the prayers over the people, numbers 2 and 5 speak of fidelity to the Lord and of being strengthened by the eucharist to live the faith.

Sunday Preface I speaks of the qualities of the Church which are needed to continue to praise the wisdom of God. Hence these two prefaces carry through the ideas of the second reading about remaining faithful to God's word.

A suitable blessing to reflect the theme of the preaching of the word is number 20 of the prayers over the people, which speaks of receiving the Good News.

Guidelines for the celebrant's introduction and comments:

INTRODUCTION

The test of a true Christian is that he lives his faith all the days of his life and that he practices what he preaches to others. May we who gather this day to hear the word of God pray for the grace of integrity to lead truly Christian lives in the coming week.

PENITENTIAL RITE

You came to preach the Good News of the Father: Lord, have mercy . . .

You came to challenge men to deeper levels of faith: Christ, have mercy . . .

You came to call your followers to the strict demand of love for one other: Lord, have mercy . . .

BEFORE THE READINGS

The problem with hypocrisy is that we can easily spot it in others, but we find it difficult to admit it in ourselves. In these readings it will be difficult to imagine that anyone else is the hypocrite if we apply the challenge of the word of God to ourselves.

BEFORE THE EUCHARISTIC PRAYER

To conform ourselves to Christ takes a lifetime of searching hearts and purifying motives. May our celebration of this eucharistic meal give us the courage we need to become faithful followers of the Lord.

THIRTY-SECOND SUNDAY IN ORDINARY TIME

It has been said that the task of a poet, an artist, or a philosopher is to make the ordinary extraordinary, and the extraordinary credible. Their task is to take the bland, the usual, the customary, and make of these experiences memorable events, or significant reason for reflection. The gifted eye of a painter sees things in reality and gives them an unreal and challenging look. A philosopher ponders man and his situation and lets him know not how things are, but what they could become. In either case the gift these people share with others is letting them see with different eyes and to hear sounds with different ears, that they may see beauty where it does not seem to be, and appreciate how things might be, and not be dejected at the way things are.

But the other side of the coin is to make the extraordinary credible; to make of apparently unrealizable ideals, meat and substance for the everyday lives of people. Such is the task of the preacher who proclaims the gospel of this Sunday. The main point of the parable is the division of the virgins according to their preparedness, but since the coming of Christ and his judgment will be the theme of the readings of the feast of Christ the King on the last Sunday of the year, the delay of the coming of the bridegroom takes on a greater significance. The punch line of the parable has the same weight as the readings about Christ coming in judgment, but what happened to the virgins during the delay is the point in question. The exhilaration and anticipation of waiting for the bridegroom is great, but in the delay some faltered. The same is the situation of the Church in any age. She has many members who turn out on the special occasions, but far fewer in the everydayness of Christianity. The boredom in faith on "ordinary" Sundays can set in because Christmas and Easter have already come this year, or are too far off to think about. The question raised by the gospel is what does the believer do in the meantime, in the ordinary time, in the almost boredom of his daily existence. Is he foolish, or is he wise? Does he forget his

Sundays in Ordinary Time 217

Lord and Master, or does his Christianity mean as much then as it does on the glory days?

The first reading from the book of Wisdom cites watchfulness as the key to a faithful religion and understanding of wisdom.

The psalm response speaks of thirsting for the living God, even in, or more accurately, especially in the low points of our lives, so that man can reach from them to the heights of his faith in God. Even in the ordinary time, faith can make the extraordinary difference.

The second theme of the Scripture reading this Sunday is from first Thessalonians where Paul addresses a practical and doctrinal problem faced by the community there. Paul had preached to them and left them with the impression that the second coming of Christ was imminent. Some died before the parousia and their concern is what has happened to them. Paul states firmly and categorically that what matters is that they interpret these events because of their faith and hope in the Lord, and that this support of the Lord is for all, those who are already dead and for those who are still alive. At the end of the reading he states that we shall all be "with the Lord unceasingly." Therefore, the hope which grounds the Christian faith is life eternal with God, and that all will come to share this same existence no matter when they die.

Since there is much contemporary debate about death, dying, and theologies of suffering, in helping people to deal with these situations, the theme of this reading may be an effective alternative for the preaching this Sunday, especially if the congregation will hear the emphasis on the last judgment as the homily topic on the feast of Christ the King.

All of the prayers for the liturgy this Sunday can be interpreted to reflect the readings of the day about living the faith with God's help even in the unromantic and more difficult situations of life. Sunday Preface IV, about the return of the Lord into glory being our share in the heavenly kingdom, and VI, about the Spirit as the foretaste of the paschal feast of heaven, reflect both scriptural themes of this Sunday: the watchfulness of the community until the Lord will come again, and the condition of those who sleep in death until the second coming of the Lord.

Of the prayers over the people, numbers 11 and 22 reflect the theme of the gospel reading as they ask that the community be aided by this celebration of the eucharist to do the will of the Father. The prayers which reflect the second reading and which speak of the life to come in which we all shall share are numbers 1 and 16.

Guidelines for the celebrant's introduction and comments:

INTRODUCTION

My brothers and sisters, we come to share in this eucharist of our salvation and in it we ask the Lord for his grace to assist our continual living of the Christian life especially in times and circumstances when we would rather avoid the demands of his Gospel.

PENITENTIAL RITE

You came to teach us the will of your Father: Lord, have mercy . . .

You came to share with us the love of the Father: Christ, have mercy . . .

You come to us this day to give us the blessing and grace of our heavenly Father: Lord, have mercy . . .

BEFORE THE READINGS

Like any other community or geographical group of people, Christianity has its own special feasts and seasons, and special occasions. The point of the gospel reading, however, speaks about the other days. Our lives of faith are not to be lived occasionally or on special days. We are called to an everyday life of faith.

BEFORE THE EUCHARISTIC PRAYER

Our prayer of praise and thanksgiving is for the salvation which Christ accomplished for us in his death and resurrection. As we share now in this sacrament of his life, may we also share in the example of our lives the faith we profess in this sacrament.

THIRTY-THIRD SUNDAY IN ORDINARY TIME

Beginning with last Sunday's gospel about the five wise and five foolish virgins, continuing this week with the three servants who cared for their master's money, and ending next week with the gospel of the final judgment, the mood and tone of the Sunday liturgy takes on a new orientation. Just as in the former lectionary where the Sundays prior to Advent took on an eschatological orientation with judgment a prominent feature, these three Sundays provide in different images the same theme of the judgment. And it is with this theme that Advent begins, for we are to be ready at all times for this judgment for we know neither the day nor the hour. There are at least two levels of interpretation for this Sunday's parable from Matthew chapter 25, the teaching as it was enunciated by Jesus himself, and the interpretation of the primitive community with their consequent allegorizing of his teaching. The illustration of three sums of money always provides a certain intrigue and suspense, and the slaves who are "industrious and reliable" are those who invest the money and make it earn more than its face value. Industry by itself does not necessarily deserve a reward, but industry with the talents which the Lord gives to each in the community requires attention if they are to be developed for the benefit of all. To bury a talent, as the servant buried the silver coins, is to misunderstand the mission one assumes when he receives a gift; for a reckoning is demanded and will be exacted by the Lord. The fact of Matthew's placing this parable between the story of the ten virgins and the explicit judgment scene of the end of time indicates his concern to relate the allegorizing of the parable to the community for which he writes. The "Lord" is Jesus, the servants are all of us, the reckoning is the final judgment, and the different results of the investment scheme are the different judgments we will receive.

Matthew is clear that all will be judged and one must grow and increase in his faith on earth, not hide it or hinder its expansion. The emphasis here is on the active involvement of the individual in encouraging and fostering growth; progress in the faith does not happen by passive toleration.

The reading from the book of Wisdom is a curious introduction to this gospel reading for the only possible point of coincidence between the two is the reward the worthy wife receives for her labors.

This may be a fortunate placement of this reading, however, since a three week exploration of the main theme of the final judgment in Matthew's Gospel may be a bit severe. The preacher can choose the first reading and speak of the vocation of the married and family life, or take the second reading along with the gospel (a curious, but happy coincidence that these should coincide this Sunday) and preach on the immanence of this judgment, that it is not merely to be relegated to the end times.

The alternative form of the opening prayer this Sunday reflects the theme of the gospel since it speaks of the first coming of the Lord Jesus and that until his second coming the Christian community serves him in faith and love, and celebrates his presence with them at the table of the eucharist.

The same Sunday prefaces recommended last Sunday are appropriate this week about the coming of the Lord: Sunday Preface IV, about the eventual return of the Lord in glory, and VI about the Spirit as a foretaste of the paschal feast of heaven.

Both the second reading and the gospel speak of continuing to do the Lord's will until his second coming, and numbers 11 and 22 of the prayers over the people reflect this same theme and give it a eucharistic orientation.

Guidelines for the celebrant's introduction and comments:

INTRODUCTION

My friends in Christ, we come together this Sunday to evaluate the ways in which we have or have not lived up to the vocation we share as Christians. Today's gospel speaks of us and our fidelity in living the life of faith when it places man under the judgment of the Son of God. May we who share this eucharist this day also share our gifts and talents with this parish community and for the good of all.

PENITENTIAL RITE

Lord Jesus, you are the eternal Son of the Father: Lord, have mercy . . .

Lord Jesus, in your word is our truth: Christ, have mercy . . .

Lord Jesus, we await your coming glory: Lord, have mercy . . .

BEFORE THE READINGS

In our world of investments, stocks, interest-bartering and speculation, the simplicity of today's gospel may prove embarrassing. Yet, the gospel is addressed to us to evaluate not how well we do in financial affairs, but rather how well we do in sharing our natural talents with the rest of this community of faith.

BEFORE THE EUCHARISTIC PRAYER

We come to praise the Father for the gift of his Son and his presence with us at this eucharist. May we also praise him for the wisdom of his word this day which invites us to watchfulness for Christ's second coming.

SUNDAY AFTER PENTECOST—TRINITY SUNDAY

The recollection of the Sunday Preface of the Holy Trinity which was prescribed for use on most Sundays of the year until very recently, "the oneness of a single person, but three persons in one single essence," is still so fresh in our minds that the celebration of the solemnity of the Trinity would seem to have to be as dry as dust and something for theologians alone. But paradoxically this difficult theological truth has been translated into the most dynamic of liturgical celebrations and feasts; it is by no means dry or stilted on the side of the theologians in any way. It is a feast about the reality of God in the real lives of men; it is about the image of God in whom we believe, but an image that is eminently believable.

The first reading from the book of Exodus is about the mediatorship of Moses to whom Yahweh revealed himself as the totally other, the unconsumed yet ominous image of the burning bush. This transcendence and otherness of God would be expected to be reflected on the feast of the Trinity, but what is revealed in the reading is Moses revealing Yahweh as a Lord "slow to anger and rich in kindness." He speaks of a God who will forgive the sins of his people. The transcendence of God in the cloud is maintained, but the immanence of God with man is equally revealed.

The second reading from second Corinthians does not describe the Lord, but rather dwells on the life of the Trinity in the Christian community. The grace, peace, and fellowship of the Trinity are to be reproduced in the communality of the Christian community, and harmony and peace are to be hallmarks of this fellowship.

The gospel completes the picture of the Trinity by presenting the revelation of Jesus to Nicodemus about God's love for the world by sending his own Son to redeem us and that faith in him leads to sanctification, not condemnation. The clear message of the readings is not one of doctrinal speculation, but an assurance of God's presence with the community of the redeemed under the guidance and inspiration of the love of God, the grace of Christ and the fellowship of the Spirit. What is far more important than defining the persons in God, is to live according to the Trinity's life-giving qualities in our lives.

The prayers for the liturgy of Trinity Sunday correspond with the dynamic concept of the opening prayer which speaks of God's revelation to his people and begs that his presence may bring the world to life in him.

The prayer over the gifts asks that through the gifts of the eucharist the community may become a perfect offering to the Father.

The prayer after communion asks that this sacrament may bring this community health of mind and body.

The Preface of the Holy Trinity is prescribed on this day but is a revision of the older one and speaks of the glory of the Trinity whom we worship at the eucharist.

Solemn Blessing for ordinary time should be used for the dismissal as it calls upon the Father in the first part of the blessing, on the Son (the Word) in the second part, and prays in the third that the Church may walk in the way of the Lord.

Guidelines for the celebrant's introduction and comments:

INTRODUCTION

My brothers and sisters, we have gathered this day to celebrate the feast of the Holy Trinity. As we come to share the grace of our Lord Jesus Christ, the love of God the Father and the fellowship of the Holy Spirit we are aware that the Trinity is by no means an abstract theological term, but is the very presence of God in our daily lives.

On this Sunday it would be appropriate to use the blessing and sprinkling of holy water as the introduction since the community has been baptized into the life of the Trinity.

As we pray that God will bless this water to renew our common baptism, may we also ask him to help us live according to that baptism aided by the grace and mercy of this eucharist.

BEFORE THE READINGS

Celebrating a feast of the unity of the Trinity may serve to remind us that we are to recommit ourselves at this eucharist to live our faith aided by the gifts of the Trinity within us.

BEFORE THE EUCHARISTIC PRAYER

As we pray to the Father through his Son and in the power of the Spirit in this eucharistic prayer, may we who receive these sacred mysteries seek to live by the unity and peace they symbolize.

SUNDAY AFTER TRINITY SUNDAY—CORPUS CHRISTI

Proclaimed apart from one another, each of the three readings assigned for the solemnity of Corpus Christi could provide a suitable and fitting reflection on what the eucharist is and its place in the life of the Church. The reading from Deuteronomy recalls to the Israelites what favors the Father worked for them in delivering them from bondage, by directing their journeying, and by feeding them on their way to the land of promise. The reading from First Corinthians informs the community that the unity symbolized by the one bread and one cup is a unity that is to be realized in the lives of the assembled community. And the reading from John 6:51-58 is the classic text of the eucharistic interpretation of this entire chapter. But one theme which is enunciated in the first reading and which is carried through in the others, and which is most important for the understanding of the eucharist is the word "remember." What Christians do when they celebrate the eucharist is recall the past, reform the present, and look toward the future.

The first reading is about the definitive past, when Yahweh fed his people with manna from on high for their years of wanderings and journeying. The reading from First Corinthians speaks no longer of the past but of the present where we share the one bread and one cup. We are to become the body of Christ in the present, and to imitate the sacrament of his body and blood we receive. And the reference at the beginning of the gospel proclamation is to the bread that the Lord will give, so that anyone who eats this bread, "shall live forever." The orientation here is on the future, the coming of the kingdom, and the bread of the kingdom is the Lord's eschatological gift to those who believe him to be the only bread of life. The eucharist is our community memorial sacrifice, recalling the past deeds of redemption, the present realization of these deeds in the sacraments of the Church, and in the future when we shall all share in the food of heaven in the kingdom of the Father. Whatever the choice of theme for this celebration, the opportunity to preach on the sacrament of the eucharist and its importance for the life of the Church should not be missed by the preacher.

The opening prayer of the liturgy presents the past, present and future aspects of the eucharist by using the word "memorial" of the suffering and death of Jesus and extending it to the future, in the kingdom where the salvation won for us will be completed. The alternative form of the prayer speaks more directly to the theme of the second reading of the broken bread as a symbol of undivided love.

The prayer over the gifts recalls the unity and peace which the eucharist signifies, and the prayer after communion links the present celebration not only with the past but also with the possession of full life in the kingdom forever.

The Preface II of the Eucharist should be used because of its clear reference to the eucharist as a memorial of past, present, and future, as well as delineating the implications of this sacrament here and now. The solemn blessing III for ordinary time reflects the life a believer should live when celebrations have ended and the work of living a Christian life begins again.

Guidelines for the celebrant's introduction and comments:

INTRODUCTION

My friends in Christ, we come to the celebration of the eucharist on this solemnity of Corpus Christi. May we who are now blessed with this water as a sign of our common baptism, realize the blessing and strength which God freely offers us as we celebrate the eucharist to renew our covenant first established at baptism.

On this Sunday the rite of the blessing and sprinkling of Holy Water should be used to link the present celebration of the eucharist with the covenant of baptism.

BEFORE THE READINGS

The celebration of the eucharist needs the proclamation of the word of God to give it proper focus and perspective. Today's readings speak of the love the Father has for us by sending us this bread of heaven to heal and strengthen us as we seek to live according to the unity and peace which this bread symbolizes.

BEFORE THE EUCHARISTIC PRAYER

May we who share this one bread and one cup, be equally eager to share each other's burdens as a sign and fulfillment of our belief in what we do at the table of the Lord's body and blood.

SOLEMNITY OF CHRIST THE KING

The very title "Christ the King" would seem to indicate that we end the liturgical year with more than a note of triumph, power, and glory. It is only fitting that we who proclaim his rule and kingdom week after week should pause this Sunday to acclaim him as the King of Kings and the Lord of Lords. And yet, this is not the point of this feast at all. For the readings do not proclaim the king of triumph and glory, of sovereignty, powerful deeds, and strict authority. The first reading instead gives us our key that the Bible would prefer to speak in terms of the imagery of the shepherd and his flock and not of a super-earthly king and his array of servants. The times may not be the best, says Ezekiel: indeed, they may be "cloudy and dark," but the king whom we acclaim this day imitates the shepherd who seeks out and finds the strays of his flock; he binds up the injured, he heals those in need of healing, and understands the misunderstood. The shepherd is the image of the king we acclaim today, the simple undramatic servant, not a reigning monarch who insists on his rights and privileges.

The second reading speaks of Christ the King as the one who gives life, a new life to men in God's sight. All were bound to sin and death in Adam according to the book of Genesis, but that sin no longer weighs on mankind because Christ has come to lavish on us a vision of life freed from the corruption of sin and death, a vision of unity and peace granted to us through Christ who is forever our way to salvation.

The third image is in the gospel where all of us are invited to participate in Christ's kingship, not by stressing or resting secure in our dignity or even in exercising the power of a monarch. Instead we are asked about how much of a shepherd we still have to become. To be a member of the Church of Christ the King is to be pledged to unity and peace, the same unity and peace which have been granted to us in Christ Jesus. We have been granted all this through him, and on this feast we are to question ourselves as to how much we have extended this to others. But the final surprise and miracle of this kingship is that even if we have not shared or kept to the kingdom's demands, we shall be forgiven in this eucharist and strengthened to begin again to renew the face of this earth according to the image and likeness of the unity and peace of Christ the King who comes as a shepherd to feed the flock of the Church.

The opening prayer of the liturgy speaks of our glorifying the Father through Christ, and the alternate form of the prayer indicates that one way of doing this is by offering to mankind the gifts that we have already received through him. The prayer over the gifts speaks specifically of the gifts of unity and peace from the eucharist, and the prayer after communion links this celebration of the eucharist to the eternal kingdom where Christ lives and rules with the Father for endless ages.

The Preface of Christ the King is prescribed for this Sunday and speaks of his kingdom of truth, life, holiness, grace, justice, love and peace, which are now shared at the eucharist with the Christian community but which need to be shared as well with the rest of mankind.

The form of the solemn blessing for the dismissal of the community should be used on this feast day and the most appropriate is number III for ordinary time since it speaks of the mercy of God, sharing his gifts with others, and walking in charity and peace.

Guidelines for the celebrant's introduction and comments:

INTRODUCTION

My friends, we gather to celebrate the solemnity of Christ our Lord and universal King. As we begin our celebration of these mysteries of the redemption he has won for us let us realize the power and wisdom of Christ to whom belongs all glory and honor from us, his chosen people.

PENITENTIAL RITE

Lord Jesus, you share with us your kingdom of truth and life: Lord, have mercy . . .

Lord Jesus, you share with us a kingdom of holiness and grace: Christ, have mercy . . .

Lord Jesus, you share with us a kingdom of justice, love, and peace: Lord, have mercy . . .

BEFORE THE READINGS

In the very beginning of the book of Genesis we are told that man shares the image and likeness of God. In today's readings that image and likeness of God is defined—a shepherd whose mercy endures forever.

BEFORE THE EUCHARISTIC PRAYER

As we acclaim Christ as our shepherd and king, we acclaim his mercy and goodness toward us at this sacrificial meal. Let us join with hearts filled with wonder and praise for to him belongs all glory and honor from us, his chosen people.